The Modern Cooks Cookbook

Trinity McNab

The Modern Cooks Cookbook

TABLE OF CONTENTS

Slow Cooker Recipes

Pressure cooker recipes
Osso bucco
Beef brisket stew
Curried chicken and vegetable pasta
Fennel pork roast
Curried lamb chops
Chilli con carne
Apricot paprika chicken
Quick beef stew
Easy paprika chicken
Chicken Recipes
Chicken nuggets
Picante chicken
Chicken nachos
Jarlsberg chicken
Baked garlic chicken
Chicken paella
Easy chicken bake
Easy chicken korma
Chicken teriyaki with noodles
Domino chicken and cheesy potato bake
Chicken and rosemary ragu
Honey mustard chicken sausage rolls
Quick chicken sausage rolls
Doritos crumbed chicken tenders
Baked honey garlic chicken
Easy baked chicken
Chicken pot pie
World best chicken
Cheese and ham chicken rolls
Prosciutto wrapped chicken breast
Cornflake chicken
Chicken dinner equals winner

Lamb pasties
Chutney lamb chops
Lamb cannelloni
Roast lamb
Lamb cutlets Kilpatrick
Moroccan lamb shanks
Poached lamb with spring vegetables
Mongolian lamb
Slow roasted lamb shanks with silverbeet
Pork Recipes
Honey glazed pork
Pork with crushed potatoes
Best ever meatloaf
Pork with apple gravy
Footy meatballs
Pork and apple meatballs
Bacon and egg pie
Saucy pork chops
Cheese and bacon puffs
Mini quiches
Potato and bacon bake
Egg and bacon pizza
Pasta Recipes
My carbonara
Macaroni pasta bake
Frugal pasta
Tuscan style pasta
Simple spaghetti
Ricotta and spinach gnocchi bake
Pizza casserole
Pasta with meatballs
15-minute carbonara pasta
Spaghetti with creamy ham sauce

Orange Banana muffins
Scones
Honey joys
Chocolate chip muffins
Snow cakes
Wicked chocolate cake
Moist banana muffins
M&M chocolate chip cookies
Choc Toblerone mousse
Baked custard
Apple cinnamon muffins
Tim tam truffles
Coconut rough slice
Apple tea cake
Cranberry and orange icy poles
Big freckles
Strawberry and cream bliss cake
Mums chocolate slice
Subway cookies
Double chocolate pancakes
Quick Nutella mousse
Ultimate mars bar slice
Lemon slice
Strawberry muffins
Milo drop balls
Peppermint bubble slice
Banana chocolate cake
Berry sundaes with white chocolate sauce
Banana and buttermilk cake
Double chocolate muffins
Triple choc muffins
Strawberry tarts
Other recipes

Easy sausage rolls
Lemon butter
Zucchini slice
Shakshuka
Spinach, feta and ricotta pie
Croque monsieur
Easy cheesy muffins
Pizza toast
Tuna melt
Chicken noodle frittata
Rice and capsicum
Mozzarella and prosciutto quesadillas
Popcorn bags
Tomato and zucchini sauce
Garlic feta dip
Chocolate icing with evaporated milk
Zucchini pickles
Wholemeal pizza dough
Loaded cheesy bacon dip
Baked eggs in ham cups
Healthy devilled eggs
Jam pinwheels
Kid friendly turkey balls
Ham and pineapple pinwheels
Garlic potato
Zucchini fritters
Butterscotch sauce
Gluten Free
Chocolate panna cotta
Sticky mango rice
3 ingredient pumpkin soup
Alfredo
Parsnip rice

Candy cane and brownie ice cream
Minted roast lamb and vegetables
Pulled maple Christmas ham
Choc-coconut Christmas balls
Christmas crackles
Gingerbread shapes

DEDICATION

This book is dedicated to my friends and family. Thank you all for being such a special part of my life and believing in me. I have always wanted to create my own cookbook, as I create a lot of recipes. I hope everyone will love this book as much as I have enjoyed writing it. May this cookbook help bring all your family and friends together to enjoy delicious food and bring happiness to everyone in the kitchen and out.

Slow Cooker Recipes

Pulled Beef

Yield: 8 serves

Ingredients

1.5kg topside beef

2 garlic cloves, crushed

2 brown onions, peeled and chopped

1/3 cup brown sugar

1 stalk rosemary

1 cup red wine

Salt and pepper to taste

Method:

1. Trim all the fat off the meat and then place in the slow cooker.
2. Season generously with salt, pepper and garlic.
3. Add the onions, brown sugar, rosemary and red wine.
4. Cover and cook on low for 8 hours or until beef is tender.
5. Use 2 forks to shred the beef apart, stirring as you go.
6. Leave it sit in the delicious sauce for at least 15 mins.

Chicken Casserole

Yield: 6-8 Serves

Ingredients:

1kg chicken thighs

1 packet frozen vegetables

1 packet chicken noodle soup mix

1 brown onion diced

3 tbsp minced garlic

1L chicken stock

1 tin condensed cream of chicken soup

Pinch of salt and pepper to taste

Method:

1. Place all the ingredients in the slow cooker and cook on low for 6-8 hours depending on size of your slow cooker.
2. Some slow cookers cook faster than others I use a 6L slow cooker.
3. Once cooked I dice the chicken and put back in and stir to combine.
4. I also sometimes serve this recipe with 2-minute chicken noodles.

Sausages with onion gravy

Yield: 5 serves

Ingredients:

2 large brown onions sliced or diced

1 cup beef stock

2 tbsp corn flour

1 garlic clove crushed

1 tbsp freshly chopped rosemary leaves

10 thin beef sausages

Method:

1. Place onions in the slow cooker.
2. In a jug combine stock, cornflour, garlic and rosemary and whisk until smooth.
3. Pour over onions.
4. Add the sausages.
5. Cook on low for 4 hours.
6. Serve with mashed potato.

McNab garlic saucy bangers.

Yield: 8-10 serves

Ingredients:

24 beef sausages

2 tins of condensed cream of mushroom soup

½ cup tomato sauce

½ cup bbq sauce

1 packet french onion soup mix

1-2 tbsp Worcestershire sauce

2-3 tbsp minced garlic

Method:

1. place sausages in the slow cooker.
2. In a separate bowl mix together the rest of the ingredients.
3. Pour over the top of the sausages and cook on low for 6-8 hours.
4. Usually, I serve with mashed potato and possibly mixed vegetables.

French lamb casserole

Yield: 4-6 serves

Ingredients:

1kg lamb forequarter chops

1 packet french onion soup mix

1 tin crushed tomatoes

6 carrots peeled and halved

You could also add other vegetables too if you did that, I would add another tin of tomatoes.

Method:

1. Place all ingredients in the slow cooker and cook on low for 6 hours or on high for 3-4 hours.

Yummo Lambo

Yield: 4-6 serves

Ingredients:

4-6 lamb forequarter chops

1 can of condensed tomato soup

1 little bit of water

1 packet french onion soup mix

2-3 tbsp Worcestershire sauce

2 tbsp mint sauce

Method:

1. Place lamb chops in the slow cooker.
2. In a bowl mix tomato soup, water, french onion soup mix, Worcestershire sauce and mint sauce together.
3. Pour on top of the lamb chops and then stir through.
4. Cook on low for 6-7 hours meat will fall off the bone.

Simple chicken tacos

Yield: 4 serves
Ingredients:
4 chicken breasts
1 small jar of salsa
½ cup of water
1 packet taco seasoning
Taco shells

Method:

1. Place all the ingredients into the slow cooker and cook on low for 6 hours.
2. Shred the chicken and serve in the taco shells with whichever topping you like.

Meatball Ragu

Yield: 4-6 serves

Ingredients:

500g beef mince

500g pork mince

1 onion finely chopped

2 garlic cloves crushed

¼ cup finely chopped parsley

1/3 cup breadcrumbs

1 egg whisked

3 400g tins diced tomatoes

3 tbsp tomato paste

4 sprigs basil leaves picked and chopped

180g fresh mozzarella roughly torn

½ cup grated parmesan

Method:

1. Combine minces, onion, garlic, parsley, breadcrumbs and egg in a bowl and mix together well using your hands.
2. Roll into large meatballs and place into slow cooker.
3. Add tomatoes, tomato paste and chopped basil and season with salt and pepper.
4. Cover and cook on low for 6 hours.
5. When ready to serve preheat grill to high.
6. Transfer meatballs and sauce into a large heatproof dish.
7. Scatter with mozzarella and parmesan and grill for 6 mins or until golden.
8. Tip: if you don't have a slow cooker, brown meatballs in a frying pan over medium heat, turning often, until well browned. Add tomatoes, paste and basil and bring to the boil. Transfer to an oven proof dish and bake in preheated oven on 180oC for 25

mins or until meatballs are cooked through. Top with cheese and bake for a further 10 mins until melted.

Jacket Potatoes

Yield: 6 serves

Ingredients:

6 potatoes

1 tbsp olive oil

Method:

1. Wash and thoroughly dry each potato.
2. Prick all potatoes all over and put in a bowl.
3. Add olive oil and rub all over potatoes to coat evenly.
4. Season well with salt and pepper and toss to coat.
5. Wrap each potato tightly in foil and put in the slow cooker in one even layer if possible.
6. Cover with lid and cook on high for 5 hours for large potatoes, turning them over hallway through the cooking time.
7. Test the potatoes are cooked by inserting a knife into the centre of the potato through the foil – it should slide in easily.
8. Lift potatoes out of the slow cooker onto a plate or board using a large spoon and carefully unwrap.
9. Serve with your choice of toppings (ham, butter, cheese, cooked bacon diced, coleslaw etc)

Honey mustard chicken

Yield: 4 serves

Ingredients:

1 tbsp olive oil

1 tsp sweet paprika

8 chicken thigh cutlets skin removed

2 rindless bacon rashers coarsely chopped

2 tbsp cornflour

2 tsp dry mustard powder

2/3 cup chicken stock

2 tbsp wholegrain mustard

1 tbsp Dijon mustard

2 tbsp honey

½ cup frozen peas thawed

2 tbsp cooking cream

2 tbsp chopped fresh flat leaf parsley leaves

Method:

1. Combine the oil and paprika in a large bowl.
2. Add chicken and toss to coat.
3. Heat a large non-stick frying pan over a medium-high heat.
4. Add chicken and cook turning for 5 mins or until browned.
5. Transfer to a plate.
6. Add bacon to pan and cook stirring for 5 mins or until golden and crisp and then transfer to plate.
7. Place the cornflour and mustard powder in a slow cooker, and gradually whisk in stock, mustards and honey until smooth.
8. Add the chicken and bacon to the cooker and gently stir to combine.
9. Cook on low for 4 hours stirring in the peas and cream in the last 10 mins of cooking.
10. Serve the chicken with sprinkled parsley.

Cheesy bacon potatoes

Yield: 4 serves

Ingredients:

1 ½ tbsp olive oil

750g baby chat potatoes halved

2 garlic cloves

3 rashers shortcut bacon cut into thin strips

½ cup grated tasty cheese

Fresh chives to serve

Method:

1. Line a slow cooker with a sheet of baking paper.
2. Add the potato, garlic and 1 tbsp of the oil.
3. Season with salt and pepper and toss to coat.
4. Cover and cook on high for 4 hours or until tender.
5. Heat the remaining oil in a frying pan over medium heat and cook the bacon stirring occasionally for 4 mins or until crisp.
6. Take the lid off the slow cooker and wipe any moisture from the underside.
7. Sprinkle the potato with the bacon and cheese.
8. Fold a clean tea towel in half ad place over the slow cooker.
9. Cover and cook for a further 20 mins or until the cheese has melted.
10. Sprinkle the potato with chopped chives to serve.

Chicken tikka masala

Yield:4 serves

Ingredients:

1kg chicken thighs cut into large pieces

2 400g cans crushed tomatoes

2 large brown onions thinly sliced

2/3 cup tikka masala curry paste

¼ cup thickened cream

1 cup coarsely chopped fresh coriander

Steamed rice to serve

Method:

1. Combine chicken, tomatoes, onion and paste in a slow cooker.
2. Cook and cover on high for 3 ½ hours.
3. Drizzle with cream and sprinkle over coriander.
4. Serve with steamed rice.

Chicken Diane

Yield: 4 serves

Ingredients:

8 chicken cutlets

2 tsp olive oil

1 brown onion finely chopped

2 garlic cloves finely chopped

2 tbsp cornflour

½ cup chicken stock

1 cup pouring cream

2/3 cup passata

1 tbsp Worcestershire sauce

1 tbsp Dijon mustard

200g button mushrooms thinly sliced

½ packet fresh egg fettucine

Parsley to serve

Method:

1. Heat a large non-stick frying pan over a high heat.
2. Season the chicken and place skin side down in the pan.
3. Cook for 3 mins or until golden.
4. Turn and cook for a further 2 mins.
5. Transfer to a slow cooker.
6. Drain the rendered fat from the pan and discard.
7. Heat oil in the frying pan.
8. Reduce heat to a medium-low and add the onion and garlic and cook stirring often for 2 mins or until soft.
9. Add to the slow cooker.
10. Meanwhile place the cornflour in a large jug and gradually whisk in the stock.
11. Add the cream, passata, Worcestershire sauce and mustard.
12. Add mixture to the slow cooker.

13. Cover and cook on low for 3 ½ hours.
14. Add the mushroom and cook for a further 20 mins.
15. Add the pasta and cook for 10 mins or until tender.
16. Sprinkle with parsley.

Potato and cheddar soup

Yield: 4 serves

Ingredients:

1 stalk celery trimmed chopped coarsely

1kg potatoes chopped coarsely

2 medium onions chopped coarsely

½ small cauliflower chopped coarsely

2 garlic cloves thinly sliced

2 cups vegetable stock

2 cups water

1 ½ cups shredded cheddar cheese

1/3 cup thickened cream

Method:

1. Place celery, potato, onion, cauliflower, garlic, stock and water in a 5-6L slow cooker.
2. Cook on low for 8 hours.
3. Add cheddar, stir until cheese melts.
4. Cool soup for 10 mins.
5. Using a stick blender blend the soup until smooth.
6. Serve soup drizzled with cream.

Bourbon glazed beef

Yield: 4 serves

Ingredients:

1 medium onion chopped finely

5 garlic cloves chopped coarsely

½ cup tomato sauce

½ cup sweet chili sauce

1/3 cup light soy sauce

½ cup bourbon

½ cup honey

1 beef roast

Method:

1. Combine onion, garlic, sauces, bourbon, and honey in a 5L slow cooker.
2. Add beef turn to coat all over in the mixture.
3. Cook on low for 6-8 hours.
4. Carefully remove beef from slow cooker and keep warm.
5. Transfer the sauce to a large frying pan and bring to the boil.
6. Boil skimming fat from the surface for 10 mins or until sauce reduces to 2 cups.
7. Spoon over beef to serve.

Homemade apple sauce

Yield: 1.3kg
Ingredients:
1.5kg fuji apples

Method:

1. Prepare the apples by coring and slicing them you don't have to peel them unless you want to.
2. Put the apples in a slow cooker with ½ cup of water.
3. Cook on low for 6 hours or until apples are soft.
4. In batches transfer the sauce to a blender and blend.
5. Be careful not to over-blend as the sauce becomes smooth quickly.
6. Store in a sterilised jar in the fridge for up to 1 month.

Mac & cheese with garlic

Yield: 4 serves

Ingredients:

1 cup diced bacon

1 ½ cup grated cheese

1 cup macaroni

1 cup warm water

1 cup milk

1 tbsp butter

2 garlic cloves crushed

½ tsp salt

Method:

1. Heat a large frying pan sprayed with cooking oil over medium-high heat.
2. Fry the bacon until crisp then transfer to a slow cooker.
3. Add the remaining ingredients and stir well to combine.
4. Cover and cook on high for 45 mins stirring every 15 mins.
5. Then turn to low and remove the lid and cook for a further 30-45 mins until the macaroni Is cooked and sauce has thickened.

Chicken with creamy mushroom rice

Yield: 4 serves

Ingredients:

1 tbsp oil

8 chicken drumsticks

2 tbsp finely chopped onion

1 garlic clove crushed

2 cups milk

420g tin condensed cream of mushroom soup

¾ cup jasmine rice

¼ cup grated parmesan cheese

2 tsp salt

1 tsp pepper

Method:

1. Heat oil in a large frying pan over a medium-high heat.
2. Brown the chicken drumsticks on all sides, remove from the pan and set aside.
3. Add the onion and garlic and fry until softened.
4. Remove from heat and mix in milk and the soup stirring until smooth.
5. Add the rice, cheese, salt and pepper.
6. Stir to combine then transfer to the slow cooker.
7. Place browned chicken on top.
8. Cook on high for 3-4 hours until the chicken is done, and the rice is tender and creamy.

Slow cooker chocolate lava cake

Yield: 6-8 serves

Ingredients:

3 ½ cups brown sugar

2 cups plain flour

6 tbsp cocoa powder

4 tsp baking powder

1 tsp salt

1 cup milk

4 tbsp butter, melted

1 tsp vanilla extract

3 cups boiling water

Vanilla ice cream or cream to serve

Method:

1. Grease a slow cooker and line with baking paper.
2. In a large bowl mix together 2 cups of the sugar, the flour, half the cocoa and the baking powder and salt.
3. Stir in the milk, melted butter and vanilla.
4. Combine the remaining brown sugar with the remaining cocoa powder and add to mixture.
5. Pour cake batter into the prepared slow cooker.
6. Pour boiling water over the top of the cake batter and resist the temptation to stir.
7. Do not stir.
8. Cover by putting a tea towel under the lid and cook on high for 2 – 2 ½ hours or until your knife or skewer comes out clean.
9. Remove the slow cooker lid and set the cake aside to cool for 30 mins before serving.
10. Serve with cream or ice cream.

Blueberry butter

Yield: 4-5 cups
Ingredients:
5 cups of blueberries pureed
1 cup sugar
2 tsp ground cinnamon
½ tsp freshly grated nutmeg (optional)
¼ tsp ground ginger
Zest of 1 lemon

Method:

1. Put the pureed blueberries in a slow cooker.
2. Cover and cook on low for 1 hour.
3. Stir the blueberry puree and prop open the slow cooker lid with a spatula or wooden spoon and continue cooking for 4 hours.
4. Add the sugar, spices and lemon zest and stir well to combine.
5. If the mixture is still a little runny remove the lid and cook uncovered on high for 1 hour or until thickened.
6. Pour into a blender or food processor and process until smooth.
7. Store in airtight containers or sterilised jars in the fridge.

Currywurst

Yield: 4 serves

Ingredients:

1 cup passata

1 cup tomato sauce

1 small onion finely chopped

1 tbsp curry powder plus extra to serve

1 tsp ground cumin

1 tsp ground paprika

8 pork sausages

Hot chips or mashed potato to serve

Method:

1. Combine passata, sauce, onion, curry powder, spices and ½ cup of water in the slow cooker then add the sausages.
2. Cook on high for 1 ½ hours.
3. Take the sausages out and cut into bite sized pieces.
4. Return to slow cooker and cook for a further 30 mins.
5. Serve sprinkled with curry powder on top along with chips or mashed potato.

Garlic and sweet chilli chicken pasta

Yield: 4 serves

Ingredients:

500g chicken breast diced

1 onion diced

1 red capsicum sliced

½ cup sweet chilli sauce

2 garlic cloves minced

300ml cooking cream

½ cup grated parmesan

Penne pasta to serve

Method:

1. Combine chicken, onion, capsicum, sweet chilli sauce and garlic in the slow cooker.
2. Cook on high for 2 hours.
3. Stir in cream and parmesan and cook for a further 1 hour.
4. Stir through cooked pasta and serve.

Caramel rice pudding

Yield: 3-4 serves

Ingredients:

¾ cup long grain rice

3 cups milk

¾ cup white sugar

½ cup caramel sauce or topping plus extra to serve

1 tsp ground cinnamon

Ice cream or cream to serve

Method:

1. Lightly grease the slow cooker.
2. Rinse the rice and place into slow cooker.
3. Add the milk, sugar, caramel sauce and cinnamon.
4. Cook on high for 2 ½ hours or until rice has absorbed most of the liquid.
5. Serve topped with extra caramel sauce and ice cream or cream.

I can't believe its chocolate cobbler

Yield: 6-8 serves

Ingredients:

180g butter melted

1 ½ cups self-raising flour

½ cup milk

2 tbsp cocoa powder

2 tsp vanilla extract

3 cups sugar

½ cup cocoa powder extra

2 ½ cups boiling water

Whipped cream, ice cream or cream to serve

Method:

1. Pour the melted butter into the bottom of the slow cooker.
2. Combine the milk, vanilla, flour, cocoa powder and 1 ½ cups of the sugar.
3. Pour mixture over the butter.
4. In a small bowl mix together the remaining sugar and extra cocoa powder.
5. Sprinkle over the batter.
6. Gently pour over the boiling water over the top and do not mix.
7. Cook on high for 3-4 hours until set.
8. Serve with whipped cream, ice cream or cream.

The best creamy, cheesy chicken and rice

Yield: 6-8 serves

Ingredients:

Cooking spray

1 ½ cups long grain brown rice

2 tsp garlic powder

2 tsp onion powder

1 tsp dried thyme

1 tsp kosher salt

700g chicken thighs cut into pieces

3 cups chicken stock

1 tbsp Dijon mustard

60g cream cheese cut into 4 pieces

1 bag frozen peas and carrots

1 cup shredded cheese

Method:

1. Grease a 6L slow cooker with cooking spray.
2. Turn on the high setting.
3. Add the rice, garlic powder, onion powder, thyme and salt.
4. Stir to combine.
5. Add chicken over the top in an even layer.
6. Whisk together the stock and mustard in a measuring cup and pour over the chicken.
7. Cover and cook on high without stirring until stock is absorbed, the rice is tender, and the chicken is cooked through 3 ½ to 4 hours.
8. Add the peas, carrot and cream cheese and stir until cream cheese is mostly melted and combined.
9. Top with shredded cheese.
10. Cover and cook until the peas are heated through, and the cheese is melted 10-15 mins and then serve.

Slow cooker Italian chicken thighs

Yield: 4 serves

Ingredients:

8 baby carrots

1 onion wedged

4 chicken thighs

1 ½ cups leggos marinara sauce

¼ cup Italian dressing

Method:

1. Place carrots and onion at the bottom of a slow cooker.
2. Top with chicken thighs.
3. Drizzle the chicken with the dressing and then the marinara sauce.
4. Cook on low for 7 hours and sprinkle with parmesan cheese if desired.

Curry chicken

Yield: 6 serves

Ingredients:

600g chicken thighs

¼ tsp salt

¼ tsp pepper

1 medium onion cut into strips

1 red capsicum cut into strips

1 large carrot diced

1 cup frozen peas

3 tbsp curry powder

1 tsp minced garlic

2 cups coconut milk

1 cup chicken stock

1 tbsp cornflour

1 tbsp water

3 cup cauliflower rice

Method:

1. Wash chicken and pat dry and season with salt and pepper.
2. Place chicken, onion, carrots, peas, capsicum, curry powder and garlic in the slow cooker.
3. Add chicken stock and coconut milk and cook on low for 4 hours.
4. Remove chicken from slow cooker and gently shred the chicken on a plate.
5. Add equal parts cornflour and water to a small mixing bowl and blend thoroughly until a paste forms.
6. While the chicken is out of the cooker add the cornflour mixture to the liquid in the cooker and stir.
7. Allow that to cook for 10 mins before adding chicken back in.
8. Continue to cook and additional hour before serving with cooked cauliflower rice.

PRESSURE COOKER RECIPES

Osso Bucco

Yield: 4 serves
1.5kg veal osso bucco
¼ cup plain flour
¼ cup olive oil
2 ½ tbsp butter
1 medium brown onion coarsely chopped
3 garlic cloves crushed
3 stalks of celery trimmed and coarsely chopped
3 large carrots coarsely chopped
3 medium tomatoes coarsely chopped
1 cup dry white wine
500ml beef stock
410g tin crushed tomatoes
3 sprigs fresh thyme
Salt and pepper to taste

Method:

1. Coat the veal in flour and shake off the excess.
2. Heat the oil in the pressure cooker.
3. Cook the veal in batches until browned all over.
4. Remove from the cooker and set aside.
5. Melt the butter in the pressure cooker, cook the onion, garlic, celery and carrot stirring until vegetables soften.
6. Add the wine to deglaze the pan.
7. Add remaining ingredients and season.
8. Return the veal to the pressure cooker, ensuring it is immersed in the liquid.

9. Close the pressure cooker and cook for 5 mins.
10. Serve with mashed potatoes and green vegetables.

Beef Brisket Stew

Yield: 6 serves

Ingredients:

900g beef brisket cut into cubes

450g beef tenderloin

6 slices fresh ginger

2 spring onions cut into 2.5cm pieces

1 tbsp oil

4 garlic cloves crushed

SAUCE

4 tbsp tomato sauce

425ml beef stock

1 tsp salt

Chinese 5 spice to taste

125g celery diced

250g carrots diced

Method:

1. Blanch beef brisket, beef tenderloin, ginger and spring onions in boiling water for 5 mins, then drain and set aside.
2. Heat a medium frying pan with 1 tbsp oil over high heat and stirfry the garlic until aromatic 2-3 mins.
3. Add the beef brisket and beef tenderloin then mix well.
4. Stir in the tomato sauce, beef stock, salt and Chinese 5 spice.
5. Add just enough hot water to cover the ingredients and bring to the boil.
6. Once boiling transfer everything into the pressure cooker.
7. Cook under high pressure for 10 mins.
8. Turn the heat off and wait until the pressure died down naturally.
9. Meanwhile simmer the celery and the carrots over medium heat for 30 mins.
10. Place into the pot with the beef.

11. Cut the beef tenderloin into large pieces and place back into the
    pot and stir to combine and serve.

Curried chicken and vegetable pasta

Yield: 4-6 serves

Ingredients:

5 chicken thighs

1 red capsicum chopped

1 green capsicum chopped

1-2 tbsp minced garlic

1 tin condensed tomato soup

1 tin diced tomatoes

½ cup bbq sauce

Good sprinkle of curry powder

150g-200g diced bacon

½ packet frozen vegetables

Use empty tomato soup tin and fill up half the can with water

Pasta

Method:

1. Place all ingredients except pasta in pressure cooker.
2. Cook on high for 40 mins.
3. While this is cooking cook pasta as per packet instructions.
4. combine with the cooked pasta and stir through.
5. Serve.

Fennel pork roast

Yield: 8 serves

Ingredients:

3 tbsp olive oil

2kg pork roast

1 pinch salt and pepper to taste

2 garlic cloves crushed

300ml white wine

300ml chicken stock

1 onion sliced

1kg fresh fennel cut into thick slices

Method:

1. Add the olive oil into the pressure cooker, season the roast with salt and pepper, brown on all sides over high heat.
2. Remove the roast from the heat and set aside on a plate.
3. Add the garlic, white wine and chicken stock to the pressure cooker.
4. Heat over high heat scraping the bottom to get the juices.
5. Put the roast back into the pressure cooker, close and cook for 45 mins.
6. After it starts to whistle, carefully open the pressure cooker to release the steam.
7. Once the steam has gone add the onion and fennel then close again and cook for another 20 mins.
8. Once done release the pressure and then remove the roast and vegetables and keep warm.
9. Put the pressure cooker sauce into a pot and reduce the sauce for several minutes.
10. If it's still too liquidy, you can add a tbsp of flour to thicken the sauce while stirring constantly.
11. Serve the roast, sauce and vegetables.

Curried lamb chops

Yield: 4 serves

Ingredients:

3 tbsp oil

2 cloves

2 cinnamon sticks

2 green cardamom pods

2 bay leaves

½ tsp black cumin seeds

2 onions sliced

3 green chillies slit lengthways

4 tsp garlic ginger paste

3 tomatoes finely diced

½ cup shredded coconut

2 tsp chilli powder

1 tsp powdered turmeric

2 tsp powdered coriander

Salt to taste

500g lamb chops

Fresh coriander

2 tsp tamarind paste

Method:

1. In a pressure cooker, heat oil and add cloves, cinnamon, cardamon pods, bay leaves and cumin seeds.
2. Let splutter, then add the sliced onions and sauté until golden brown.
3. Add the slit green chillies, garlic and ginger paste, diced tomatoes and sauté for 2 mins.
4. Add the shredded coconut and the spices: chilli powder, turmeric, coriander and salt.
5. Add the lamb chops and sauté for 10 mins.

6. Add ½ cup water and a handful of coriander leaves and put lid on pressure cooker.
7. Cook on medium pressure until it whistles.
8. Let it rest, the release the steam and remove the lid.
9. Heat the pressure cooker again without the lid.
10. Add the tamarind paste and a little more coriander and bring to a simmer.
11. Serve.

Chilli con carne

Yield: 6 serves

Ingredients:

500g beef mince

2 tsp olive oil

1 onion chopped

1 small green capsicum finely chopped

1 red chilli seeded and finely chopped

2 garlic cloves minced

2 cans red kidney beans drained and rinsed

2 cans diced tomatoes

3 tbsp tomato paste

1 tbsp dark brown sugar

2 tsp unsweetened cocoa

¼ tsp chilli flakes or to taste

2 tbsp chilli powder

2 tsp ground cumin

½ tsp salt or to taste

2 cups water

Method:

1. Place the beef mince in the pressure cooker over medium high heat and cook until brown and crumbly 8-10 mins.
2. Remove the beef mince and drain off excess fat.
3. In a frying pan pour in olive oil over medium heat stir in onion, green capsicum and red chilli.
4. Cook and stir for 3-4 mins until onion is translucent.
5. Add the garlic and cook and stir for another 30 seconds.
6. Place into pressure cooker with meat, mix in the kidney beans, diced tomatoes, tomato paste, brown sugar, cocoa, chilli flakes, chilli powder, cumin, salt and water.

7. Lock the lid bring the cooker up to pressure reduce heat to maintain pressure and cook for 8 mins.
8. Once done let the steam release naturally.
9. When the pressure is released, remove the lid, stir and serve.

Apricot Paprika sauce chicken

Yield: 4 serves

Ingredients:

1 tbsp olive oil

1 ½ kg chicken pieces

Salt and pepper to taste

½ tsp paprika

½ tsp dried marjoram

¼ cup white wine

¼ cup chicken stock

Apricot sauce:

¼ cup apricot jam

2 tbsp white vinegar

1 ½ tsp finely chopped fresh ginger

2 tbsp honey

Method:

1. Heat the olive oil in the pressure cooker with the lid off over medium-high heat.
2. Add chicken and brown on all sides as evenly as possible.
3. Remove the chicken from the cooker and season with salt, pepper, paprika and marjoram.
4. Drain and discard fat from the cooker and mix in wine and chicken stock scraping any bit of food that are stuck to the bottom.
5. Mix together the sauce ingredients.
6. Return chicken to the cooker over a medium-high heat, pour the sauce ingredients over, secure the lid and bring to high pressure for 8 mins or until chicken is tender.
7. Reduce pressure before opening lid.
8. Remove chicken pieces to a serving dish with a slotted spoon.

9. Bring sauce to a boil and cook uncovered until the sauce has reduced into a thick and syrupy consistency, about 10 mins.

10. Spoon over the chicken and serve.

Quick beef stew

Yield: 8 serves

Ingredients:

1 tbsp olive oil

1 small onion diced

1kg gravy beef

1 cup beef stock

1 cup water

3 carrots peeled and diced

2 tsp salt or to taste

8 medium potatoes peeled and diced

2 tsp cornflour

Method:

1. Heat the oil in the bottom of the pressure cooker over a medium-high heat.
2. Add the onion and beef and cook until browned on the outside.
3. Stir in the stock, water, carrots and salt, close the lid.
4. Heat until you start to hear sizzling, then reduce the heat to medium and set your timer for 20 mins.
5. Meanwhile place potatoes in a saucepan with enough water to cover.
6. Bring to the boil and cook until tender about 10 mins then drain.
7. This whole process should take about the same amount of time as the rest of the stew.
8. When the 20 mins is up, release the pressure from the cooker.
9. Remove the lid and place the ingredients in a pot and bring to the boil.
10. Stir cornflour into a small amount of cold water until dissolved.
11. Stir this into the stew and cook for a few mins.
12. Add the potatoes to the stew or place them into the serving dishes and ladle the stew over them.

Easy Paprika chicken

Yield: 4 serves

Ingredients:

4 chicken breasts halved

1 medium onion

2 tbsp plain flour

1 cup chicken stock

1 tbsp tomato paste

1 garlic clove finely chopped

1 tbsp paprika

½ tsp salt

½ tsp dried thyme

A dash of tabasco sauce

1 cup sour cream

Method:

1. Put the chicken in the pressure cooker, sprinkle the onion on top.
2. In a small bowl combine flour, and stock until smooth.
3. Whisk in the tomato paste, garlic, paprika, salt, thyme and tabasco.
4. Pour over the chicken.
5. Close lid and place pressure cooker regulator on vent pipe.
6. Bring cooker to low pressure over a high heat.
7. Reduce heat to medium-high and cook for 12 mins.
8. Remove from heat.
9. Immediately release pressure.
10. Remove chicken and keep warm.
11. Stir sour cream into cooking juices the serve over chicken.

CHICKEN RECIPES

Chicken nuggets

Yield: serves 4

Ingredients:

450g chicken breast fillets cut into bite size pieces

1 cup breadcrumbs

¾ cup mayonnaise

1 tbsp butter melted

Method:

1. Preheat oven to 180oC and line a baking tray with baking paper.
2. Coat the chicken with mayonnaise and roll in breadcrumbs.
3. Drizzle with butter and bake for 20 mins.

Picante chicken

Yield: 6 serves

Ingredients:

6 chicken breasts

2 cups salsa

1/3 cup brown sugar

2 tbsp honey Dijon mustard

Red capsicum strips

Method:

1. Preheat oven to 175oC.
2. Combine all ingredients in an ovenproof dish.
3. Bake well until the chicken is cooked about 40-45 mins.

Chicken nachos

Yield: 6 serves

Ingredients:

200g corn chips

1 cup shredded cheese

2 cups shredded roast chicken

4 tbsp bbq or sweet chilli sauce

Method:

1. Preheat oven to 170oC.
2. Spready layer of corn chips over an ovenproof plate or tray.
3. Set aside ½ cup of cheese.
4. Sprinkle the chips with some of the chicken and some of the remaining cheese, followed by a squirt of sauce.
5. Continue layering the top of everything with the reserved ½ cup of cheese.
6. Place in the oven for 10 mins or until cheese has melted.

Jarlsberg Chicken

Yield: 4 serves

Ingredients:

6 chicken breasts

6 slices of Jarlsberg cheese

2 cans condensed cream of chicken soup

6 tbsp milk

Method:

1. Preheat oven to 150oC.
2. Arrange chicken in a single layer in a casserole dish and cover with cheese.
3. Mix together the soup and milk and pour over the chicken.
4. Season and bake for 1 hour.

Baked garlic chicken

Yield: 4 serves

Ingredients:

6 garlic cloves minced

2 tbsp olive oil

1 cup brown sugar

4 chicken breasts halved

Method:

1. Preheat oven to 200oC.
2. Lightly grease a baking dish.
3. In a small frying pan, sauté the garlic in the oil until tender about 30 secs.
4. Remove from heat and stir in the brown sugar.
5. Place the chicken breasts in the baking dish and cover with the garlic and brown sugar mixture.
6. Season with salt and pepper.
7. Bake uncovered for 20 mins.

Chicken paella

Yield: 4 serves

Ingredients:

4 chicken thighs coarsely chopped

1 tbsp Portuguese seasoning or Cajun seasoning

400g can diced tomatoes

2 250g packets of microwavable brown and wild rice mix

300g packet frozen stirfry vegetables thawed

Method:

1. Combine the chicken and seasoning in a large bowl.
2. Heat a non-stick frying pan over a high heat.
3. Add half the chicken and cook, turning occasionally for 5 mins or until brown all over.
4. Transfer to a bowl.
5. Repeat with remaining chicken.
6. Return all chicken to the pan with the tomatoes.
7. Bring to a simmer.
8. Stir in rice mixture and vegetables.
9. Cook, tossing occasionally for 5-7 mins or until rice and vegetables are heated through.

Easy chicken Bake

Yield" 4-6 serves

Ingredients:

1 jar leggos tomato, spinach and ricotta bake sauce

4 chicken breasts diced

1 cup tasty, shredded cheese

Optional is 2 cups of cooked pasta

Method:

1. Preheat oven to 180oC.
2. Cook chicken in a frying pan until golden and cooked through.
3. Once cooked place chicken in an ovenproof dish.
4. Stir through the jar of sauce to cover all the chicken.
5. Add cheese over the top and cook in the oven for about 20-30 mins or until cheese is all melted and golden.

Easy chicken korma

Yield: 4-6 serves
Ingredients:
1 jar of pataks korma sauce
4 chicken breasts
Rice to serve

Method:

1. Bring a medium to large saucepan with salted water to the boil and add rice.
2. Cook rice as per packet instructions.
3. Cut up chicken into pieces and cook on a medium-high heat in a frying pan until cooked through and golden.
4. Add korma sauce and stir through to coat the chicken for 5-10 mins let it simmer.
5. Once rice is cooked drain if there is any excess water and serve in a bowl topped with the chicken korma.

Chicken Teriyaki with noodles

Yield: 4-6 serves

Ingredients:

4 chicken breasts cut into chunks

4 tbsp dark soy sauce plus extra to serve

4 tbsp mirin

2 tbsp caster sugar

250g soba noodles

Sesame oil to serve

Method:

1. Place chicken chunks into a shallow dish.
2. Combine the soy sauce, mirin, and sugar and add to the chicken and toss to coat well.
3. Set aside for 15 mins.
4. Meanwhile cook the noodles according to packet instructions.
5. Drain and fresh noodles in iced water, drain and then chill.
6. Thread chicken onto metal skewers and grill for 2-3 mins on each side.
7. Toss the noodles in a little sesame oil and serve the chicken and extra sesame oil and soy sauce.

Domino chicken and cheesy potato bake

Yield: 6 serves

Ingredients:

1.5kg medium potatoes peeled and cut into 0.3cm thick slices

1 tbsp rice bran oil

1 brown onion finely chopped

1 carrot peeled and finely chopped

2 celery sticks finely chopped

800g skinless thigh fillets coarsely chopped

3 tbsp butter plus extra melted

3 tbsp flour

1 cup chicken stock

300ml thickened cream

300g medium bacon rashers cut into 4

250g fresh mozzarella thinly sliced

Method:

1. Preheat oven to 200oC.
2. Lightly grease a 4L rectangle baking dish.
3. Place potatoes in a large saucepan and cover with cold water.
4. Bring to the boil and cook for 1-2 mins until just tender, drain and set aside to cool.
5. Heat oil in a large frying pan over a medium-high heat and add onions, carrots and celery and cook for 2-3 mins or until softened.
6. Add the chicken and cook for 2-3 mins or until golden.
7. Transfer to a bowl and set aside.
8. Add the butter and flour to the frying pan and stir to combine.
9. Pour in stock and cream and bring to the boil.
10. Cook stirring constantly until smooth.
11. Return the chicken and vegetables to the pan and stir to combine.
12. Spoon mixture into prepared baking dish.

13. Arrange a few slices of potato, 1-2 pieces of bacon and a slice of mozzarella in an alternating pattern over the top of the chicken mixture in rows.

14. Brush with melted butter and bake for 60-65 mins or until cheese is golden and sauce is bubbling.

Chicken and rosemary ragu

Yield: 4 serves

Ingredients:

2 tbsp olive oil

6 chicken thigh cutlets skin removed

1 brown onion halved and thinly sliced

2 garlic cloves thinly sliced

½ cup dry white wine

700g bottle tomato passata

1 cup chicken stock

2 bay leaves

1 tbsp chopped rosemary

¼ cup chopped parsley leaves

Cooked pappardelle pasta to serve

Grated parmesan to serve

Method:

1. Heat half the oil in a large frying pan over a medium high heat and season chicken with salt and pepper.
2. Cook chicken in batches for 4-5 mins or until browned all over.
3. Transfer to a plate.
4. Heat remaining oil in pan and add onion.
5. Reduce heat to a medium-low heat and cook stirring often for 5 mins or until golden then add garlic and cook for 1 min or until fragrant.
6. Increase heat to high and add wine and let simmer for 2 mins or until reduced.
7. Add passata, stock, bay leaves and rosemary and then return the chicken and any juices to pan.
8. Reduce heat to medium- low and simmer partially covered for 1 hour and 20 mins or until chicken is falling off the bone.
9. Remove chicken from pan and let cool for 10 mins.

10. Remove chicken from bones and discard the bones and shred the chicken into large pieces.
11. Return chicken to the sauce mixture in the pan and cook over medium heat for 5 mins or until heated through.
12. Remove and discard bay leaves and stir in parsley.
13. Toss through cooked pasta and sprinkle with parmesan.

Honey mustard chicken sausage rolls

Yield: serves 30 rolls

Ingredients:

2 500g packets chicken sausages

2 tbsp honey

1 tbsp wholegrain mustard

2 tsp Dijon mustard

¼ cup dried breadcrumbs

2 tsp thyme leaves

3 sheets frozen puff pastry just thawed

1 egg lightly whisked

Method:

1. Preheat oven to 220oC.
2. Line 2 baking trays with baking paper.
3. Remove the sausage meat from the casings and place the sausage meat in a bowl.
4. Add the honey, wholegrain and Dijon mustard, breadcrumbs and thyme and mix well until combined.
5. Cut the pastry sheets in half and arrange 1/6th of the chicken mixture lengthways down the centre of each pastry piece.
6. Brush 1 long edge of pastry with a little egg and fold the pastry over the filling to seal and form a roll.
7. Cut each roll into 5 pieces evenly and place pieces seam side down on the prepared trays.
8. Bake for 25-30 mins or until golden and cooked through and serve sausage rolls when hot.

Quick chicken sausage rolls

Yield: makes 12

Ingredients:

2 sheets frozen puff pastry just thawed

4 chicken sausages

24 baby spinach leaves

1 lightly beaten egg

Bbq sauce or tomato sauce to serve

Method:

1. Preheat oven to 190oC.
2. Line a baking tray with non-stick baking paper.
3. Place puff pastry on a flat surface and cut in half.
4. Snip the end off the sausages and squeeze out the sausage mince in a straight line across the middle of each pastry strip on the longest side and top with a couple of baby spinach leaves.
5. Roll up pastry to form a long tube, trim the edges then cut each tube into 3 pieces.
6. Place the sausage rolls on the prepared tray and brush lightly with egg.
7. Bake for 15 mins or until golden and cooked through.
8. Remove from oven and set aside for 5 mins then serve with sauce.

Doritos crumbed chicken tenders

Yield: 4 serves

Ingredients:

500g chicken tenderloins halved crossways

1 cup buttermilk

170g packet nacho cheese Doritos coarsely chopped

1 egg lightly whisked

1/3 cup plain flour

Mils salsa to serve

Method:

1. Place the chicken in a glass bowl and cover with the buttermilk.
2. Cover and place in the fridge for 4 hours or overnight to marinate.
3. Preheat oven to 180oC and line a baking tray with baking paper.
4. Pulse the corn chips in a food processor until coarsely chopped and transfer to a plate.
5. Place the egg in a shallow bowl.
6. Place the flour on a separate plate.
7. Drain the chicken and discard the buttermilk.
8. Place the chicken in the flour shaking to remove the excess.
9. Dip in the egg and then press into the corn chips, pressing well to coat.
10. Transfer to the prepared tray, spray with oil and bake for 12-15 mins or until golden.
11. Serve with salsa.

Baked honey garlic chicken

Yield: 4 serves

Ingredients:

4 chicken breasts

½ tsp salt

¼ tsp black pepper

Honey garlic sauce:

2/3 cup honey

¼ cup chicken stock

2 tbsp soy sauce

2 tbsp minced garlic

1 tbsp apple cider vinegar

¼ tsp salt

1 tbsp cornflour

Method:

1. Preheat oven to 220oC.
2. Place chicken breasts on a cutting board and cover with a piece of cling wrap.
3. Use a rolling pin to flatten the thick ends of the breasts so that they are roughly the same thickness.
4. Place chicken breasts in a baking dish and season with salt and pepper.
5. Bake for 10 mins.
6. Meanwhile whisk together the sauce ingredients: honey, stock, soy sauce, garlic, vinegar, salt, and cornflour.
7. After chicken has cooked for 10 mine remove from the oven and pour the sauce over the top.
8. Bake for another 10-12 mins until the thickest part of the chicken is cooked.
9. Cover the chicken and allow to rest for 10 mins before serving.

Easy baked chicken

Yield: serves 6

Ingredients:

5-6 chicken breasts

2 tbsp olive oil

½ tsp paprika

1 tsp Italian seasoning

1 tsp salt

1 tsp pepper

method:

1. Preheat oven to 200oC.
2. Place the chicken breast in a baking dish.
3. Drizzle with olive oil over the chicken.
4. Combine seasoning in a bowl and then rub the seasoning all over the chicken breasts.
5. Bake uncovered for 25-30 mins or until chicken is cooked.
6. Remove from oven and allow to rest for 5 mins before slicing.

Chicken pot pie

Yield: serves 4-6

Ingredients:

2 sheets puff pastry

1 chicken breast

1 onion diced

1 small carrot diced

1 stick of celery diced

1 tin condensed cream of chicken soup

Method:

1. Preheat oven to 200oC.
2. Cook the chicken fillet in frying pan, remove from pan and set aside to cool.
3. Sauté the onion, carrot and celery in the pan the chicken was cooked in being sure to scrape up the browning.
4. When the chicken is cool shred the meat with a fork and add to the pan with the vegetables and stir in the cream of chicken soup and mix gently until well combined.
5. Grease a pie dish and line the base with one sheet of pastry.
6. Add the filling and top with the second sheet of pastry.
7. Trim and crimp the edges to seal either with a fork or using your fingers to pinch the edges closed.
8. Cut four or five vents in the top of the pie and brush with a little water.
9. Sprinkle with sesame seeds if desired and cook in a hot oven for 25-30 mins or until golden brown on top and base is cooked through.

World's best chicken

Yield: 4 serves
Ingredients:
4 chicken breast fillets
½ cup Dijon mustard
¼ cup maple syrup
1 tbsp red wine vinegar
Salt and pepper to taste
Fresh rosemary

Method:

1. Preheat oven to 220oC.
2. In a small bowl whisk together the mustard, syrup and vinegar.
3. Place chicken breasts into a lined baking dish.
4. Season with salt and pepper.
5. Pour mustard mixture over the chicken.
6. Make sure each breast is coated.
7. Put some more pepper on if you need to.
8. No need to marinate.
9. Bake for 30-40 mins or until meat is cooked.
10. Season with rosemary.

Cheese and ham chicken rolls

Yield: 2 serves

Ingredients:

2 chicken breast fillets

2 pieces of tasty cheese

2 pieces of sliced ham

1 tbsp wholegrain mustard

Method:

1. Preheat oven to 180oC.
2. Using a rolling pin flatten the chicken before smearing with mustard.
3. Lay a piece of cheese followed by a piece of ham on each piece of chicken.
4. Roll up and secure with a toothpick.
5. Bake for 20 mins or until browned and cooked through.
6. Remove toothpick and cut into rounds to serve.

Prosciutto wrapped chicken breast

Yield: 4-6 serves

Ingredients:

4 chicken breasts halved

8 thin slices of prosciutto

Dried thyme

Salt and pepper

Olive oil spray

Method:

1. Preheat oven to 220oC.
2. Dry chicken breast.
3. Sprinkle each chicken breast with thyme, salt and pepper.
4. Wrap a pieces of prosciutto around each chicken breast and secure with a toothpick.
5. Place on a lined baking tray and spray with cooking spray.
6. Cook chicken in oven for 15-20 mins.

Cornflake chicken

Yield: 4 serves

Ingredients:

1 cup mayonnaise

2 cups cornflakes slightly crushed

8 chicken thighs

Cooking spray

Method:

1. Pour the mayo into a bowl and the crushed cornflakes onto a plate.
2. Roll each chicken thigh into the mayo and cover well then roll in the cornflakes.
3. Refrigerate for 30 mins.
4. Preheat oven to 200oC and spray a shallow baking tray with plenty of cooking spray.
5. Bake the chicken for 40 mins or until they are cooked all the way through.
6. Season with salt and pepper to serve.

Chicken dinner equals winner

Yield: 4-6 serves

Ingredients:

1.8kg whole chicken cut into 6 pieces

2 tsp thyme leaves

2 tsp sea salt flakes plus extra to serve

¼ cup extra virgin olive oil

2 sweet potatoes peeled and cut into 1cm rounds

1 tbsp rosemary leaves

Method:

1. Place the chicken, thyme, salt and 1 tbsp olive oil in a bowl and mix using clean hands until chicken is coated.
2. Place in the fridge until ready to use.
3. Preheat oven to 220oC.
4. Line a large roasting pan with baking paper.
5. Place the sweet potato, rosemary, and the remaining oil in the prepared pan.
6. Sprinkle with extra salt and toss to coat using tongs.
7. Arrange potato rounds in an even layer and roast for 15 mins,
8. Remove the pan from the oven and using tongs place the chicken pieces on top of the potato skin side up.
9. Return to the oven and roast for another 35 mins or until chicken is golden and cooked through.
10. Remove the pan from the oven and serve the chicken and sweet potato with a salad or steamed vegetables.

Chicken parmy balls

Yield: depends on how big or small you make the balls

Ingredients:

500g chicken mince

½ breadcrumbs

2 tbsp red onion finely chopped

1 tbsp parsley chopped

495g jar pasta sauce

½ cup parmesan

Cooked pasta to serve

Method:

1. In a large bowl, mix the mince, breadcrumbs, onion, parsley and half the parmesan.
2. Season with sea salt and cracked pepper.
3. Form into balls.
4. When the mixture is all gone, add to a frying pan and over a medium heat cook until just golden.
5. Add the pasta sauce, reduce heat and simmer for 15 mins.
6. Serve with the remaining parmesan and can serve with cooked pasta.

Pizza chicken

Yield: 2-4 serves

Ingredients:

2 chicken breasts

1 cup tomato sauce

Garlic powder

Onion powder

Italian seasoning

Salt and pepper

2/3 cup pizza blend cheese

3 tbsp mini pepperoni

Method:

1. Preheat oven to 200oC.
2. Make incisions in the chicken "Hasselback style", about ½ inch apart being careful not to cut all the way through the chicken.
3. Spoon about half the tomato sauce into an even layer on the bottom of a baking dish.
4. Top with chicken and spoon the remaining sauce on top of the chicken and in between the chicken slices.
5. Sprinkle garlic powder, onion powder, Italian seasoning and salt and pepper on top of the chicken.
6. Bake for 20-25 mins or until nearly cooked through.
7. Sprinkle cheese on top of chicken and in between chicken slices.
8. Top with mini pepperoni.
9. Bake an additional 5-10 mins or until chicken is cooked through and cheese is melted.

One pot creamy garlic herb chicken

Yield: 4 serves

Ingredients:

8 chicken thighs

8 garlic cloves peeled

1 tsp dried rosemary

½ tsp dried basil

½ tsp dried oregano

400ml thickened cream

¼ cup grated parmesan cheese

½ cup white wine

Salt and pepper to taste

Method:

1. Heat frying pan on medium heat and lightly spray pan with olive oil spray.
2. Add chicken pieces and seasoning and cook for 6 mins on each side.
3. Remove from pan and cover.
4. Add garlic, lightly fry for 3 mins and add herbs.
5. Cook for 30 secs to release the flavour.
6. Add white wine and cook for 1 min.
7. Add cream, gently bring to the boil and reduce heat to low.
8. Add chicken back into the pot and add parmesan cheese.
9. Place lid on and cook until sauce thickens.
10. Season to taste.
11. Serve with your favourite veggies and mashed potato.

Creamy chicken and spinach bake

Yield: 6 serves

Ingredients:

2 cups diced cooked chicken breast

1 cup of baby spinach

½ cup sour cream

½ cup mayo

1 cup shredded mozzarella

¼ cup parmesan cheese

2 tsp garlic powder

Method:

1. Preheat oven to 180oC.
2. Steam spinach, draining any excess water.
3. Combine sour cream, mayo, cheese and garlic powder.
4. Spray baking dish with cooking spray.
5. Pour half the mixture into the baking dish.
6. Top with chicken and spinach, then pour the remaining mixture on top.
7. Bake for 45 mins.

Chicken breast rolled with ham and cheese

Yield: 4 serves

Ingredients:

4 chicken breasts pounded into 5mm thickness

125g Swiss cheese slices

125g ham sliced thin

2 tbsp grated parmesan

1 ½ tsp paprika

½ tsp garlic salt

½ tsp dried tarragon

½ tsp dried basil leaves

1 tbsp butter melted

1/3 cup breadcrumbs

Method:

1. Place chicken breasts on a baking tray.
2. Place Swiss cheese and ham slices on top and roll up securing with toothpicks if necessary.
3. In a small bowl combine the parmesan cheese, paprika, garlic salt, tarragon, basil, and breadcrumbs.
4. Mix together and dip chicken rolls in mixture to coat.
5. Drizzle with melted butter and cook on high in microwave for 4 mins or until chicken is cooked through and juices run clear.

Honey and soy chicken wings

Yield: 4 serves

Ingredients:

2kg chicken wings

½ cup honey

¾ cup soy sauce

1 garlic cloves crushed

Sesame seeds optional

Method:

1. Combine honey, soy sauce, garlic and sesame seeds in a small bowl and mix.
2. Place chicken in a container then pour marinade over the top and toss chicken to coat.
3. Chill for 1 hour.
4. Preheat oven to 215oC.
5. Place chicken on a baking tray so as not to sit in own juices during cooking.
6. Cook in oven for 20 mins.
7. Turn chicken pieces over and spoon left over marinade on the chicken.
8. Return to oven and cook for a further 25 mins.

Chicken meatballs with 3 cheeses

Yield: 6 serves

Ingredients:

750g chicken mince

2 tbsp onion minced

2 tsp ground cloves

¼ cup ricotta cheese

¼ cup mozzarella shredded

½ cup grated parmesan

3 tbsp tomato sauce

1 tbsp fresh basil chopped

2 tsp dried parsley

2 eggs beaten

Breadcrumbs for rolling meatballs in

Method:

1. In a large bowl combine the chicken, onion, cloves, ricotta cheese, mozzarella cheese, parmesan, tomato sauce, basil, parsley and eggs.
2. Mix well and form about 30 meatballs out of the mixture.
3. Roll balls in extra parmesan and breadcrumbs.
4. Heat oil in a large frying pan over medium-high heat and fry meatballs until golden brown. For 15-20 mins.

BEEF RECIPES

Chop suey

Yield: 4 serves

Ingredients:

500g beef mince

1 large onion

½ cabbage

1 packet chicken soup

2 carrots

2 cups frozen beans

Soy sauce to serve

2 tsp Curry to taste

½ cup rice

2-3 cups water

Method:

1. Use a pot to brown mince with some water then strain the mince.
2. Place mince back into pot with 2-3 cups of warm water and chicken soup.
3. Dice carrots, chop onion and cabbage then add to the pot with beans, soy sauce and curry.
4. Simmer and allow to cook for 1 ½ hours.
5. Serve with cooked rice.

Pizza casserole

Yield: 4-6 serves

Ingredients:

2 cups uncooked egg noodles

250g beef mince

1 onion chopped

2 garlic cloves minced

1 green capsicum chopped

1 cup pepperoni sliced

480ml pizza sauce

4 tbsp milk

1 cup shredded mozzarella cheese

Method:

1. Cook noodles according to packet instructions.
2. Preheat oven to 175oC.
3. In a medium frypan over a medium-high heat, brown the mince with onion, garlic and capsicum.
4. Drain the excess fat.
5. Stir in noodles, pepperoni, pizza sauce and milk then mix well.
6. Transfer to a casserole dish.
7. Bake in the oven for 20 mins.
8. Remove from oven, top with cheese, and bake for a further 10 mins or until cheese is melted.

Lasagne

Yield: 8 serves

Ingredients:

2kg beef mince

Masterfoods Bolognese herbs

3 jars of raguletto Bolognese sauce

2-3 tbsp minced garlic

Pinch of salt

2 tsp sugar

2 packets lasagne sheets

4 jars of dolmio bechamel sauce

Shredded tasty cheese

Method:

1. In a large frying pan brown, the mince.
2. Add Bolognese herbs and stir through.
3. Add the garlic and stir through until fragrant and then add the Bolognese sauce, salt and sugar then stir to combine.
4. Let simmer for 5-10 mins.
5. Preheat oven to 180oC.
6. Use a large ovenproof dish and grease with cooking oil.
7. Place lasagne sheets on the bottom to make the first layer, the spoon over some of the Bolognese sauce, then on top of the Bolognese sauce add some bechamel sauce.
8. Repeat this for another 2 layers.
9. With the last layer I put lasagne sheets on then I put the meat, then the bechamel and then cover with shredded cheese.
10. Bake in the oven for 30 mins and until cheese is all melted and golden.
11. Serve with chips or a salad.

Easy beef stirfry

Yield: 4-6 serves

Ingredients:

2 packets coles beef stirfry strips

1 packet of coles family stirfry vegetable mix

1 small jar of oyster sauce

Method:

1. Brown the beef in a wok or a frying pan.
2. Once beef is cooked pour the vegetable packet mix and cook until slightly soft.
3. Stir in oyster sauce and continue to cook stirring for a few mins.
4. Serve with rice or eat on its own.

Mince steak stew

Yield: 6-8 serves

500g beef mince

1 large onion

½ packet of mixed vegetables

1 tsp salt

1-2 cups water or just enough to cover

1 tin crushed tomatoes

2 tbsp Worcestershire sauce

Cornflour to thicken at the end

Method:

1. Brown mince in a little water then strain the mince.
2. Place in pot with chopped onion, tomatoes and mixed vegetables.
3. Add salt with warm water then bring to the boil, then turn down the heat so stew simmers and allow to cook for 1 ½ hours.
4. When cooked thicken with cornflour and water.
5. Serve with mashed potato or on its own.

Super easy Mongolian beef

Yield: 4 serves

Ingredients:

700g steak sliced thin

¼ cup cornflour

3 tbsp vegetable oil

½ cup soy sauce

½ cup brown sugar

¼ cup water

1 tsp minced ginger

3 garlic cloves minced

Pinch of red pepper flakes

Spring onions for garnish

Method:

1. In a large Ziplock bag, add the sliced steak and cornflour.
2. Toss the beef to coat evenly.
3. Heat a large frying pan to high heat and add the vegetable oil.
4. Once heated, add the steak in a single layer and cook on each side for about 1 min until edges just start to brown.
5. Once the steak is cooked, remove and set aside on a plate.
6. In a small mixing bowl combine soy sauce, brown sugar, water, ginger and garlic.
7. Add the sauce to the pan and bring to the boil.
8. Add the steak to the sauce and allow the sauce to thicken for a couple of mins.
9. Toss with the chopped spring onions and sprinkle with red pepper flakes.

Tomato meatballs

Yield: 4-6 serves

Ingredients:

500g beef mince

1 onion diced

½ cup rice cooked

2 tbsp plain flour

1 pinch of salt and pepper

1 egg beaten

2 tins condensed tomato soup

Water

Method:

1. Combine mince, onion, rice, flour, salt and pepper in a bowl.
2. Add beaten egg and mix well.
3. With floured hands, roll into balls using about 2 tbsp for each one.
4. TIP: kids like to help roll the balls it can be messy but a super fun thing to do together in the kitchen.
5. Mix tomato soup with half a can of water.
6. Bring to the boil in a large frying pan.
7. Place meatballs in a single layer, place lid on frying pan and gently simmer for an hour and turn occasionally.

Devilled beef

Yield: 4-6 serves

Ingredients:

1kg gravy beef

1/3 cup tomato sauce

2 tbsp vinegar

1 tbsp Worcestershire

1 tbsp brown sugar

2 tsp seeded mustard

2 tsp lemon juice

2 tsp sherry

1 ½ tsp salt

3 tsp cornflour

Mashed potato and vegetables to serve

Method:

1. Remove all visible fat from beef and cut into pieces.
2. Mix together the tomato sauce, vinegar, Worcestershire sauce, brown sugar, mustard, lemon juice, sherry and salt.
3. Pour 3 tbsp of the mixture over the base of the slow cooker and place the beef on top.
4. Pour remaining liquid over the beef.
5. Cook on high for 4-5 hours.
6. Meanwhile mix the cornflour with about 2 tbsp cold water to make a paste.
7. Remove the meat and pour the juices into a small saucepan.
8. Cook over high heat until it has reduced to about half of the original volume.
9. Thicken with a little or all of the cornflour.
10. Add salt and pepper to taste.
11. Return meat to the sauce and cook on high for a few mins.
12. Serve with mashed potatoes and vegetables.

Steak Normanby

Yield: 8 serves

Ingredients:

2kg gravy beef cut into bite size pieces

2 tbsp plain flour

2 tsp sugar

3 large brown onions sliced into rings

1 tbsp crushed garlic

1 tbsp Worcestershire sauce

2 tbsp tomato sauce

2 tbsp white vinegar

½ cup beef stock

3 bacon rashers thinly sliced

Method:

1. Preheat oven to 180oC.
2. Place beef in a plastic bag with the flour and sugar and shake to coat well.
3. Line the bottom of a deep casserole dish with ¾ of the onion rings and sprinkle with the garlic over the top.
4. Place the floured meat on top of that.
5. In a large bowl mix the sauces, vinegar, and stock and pour carefully over the meat.
6. Then top with the bacon and remaining onion.
7. Cover and cook for 2 ½ hours.
8. Take the lid off for the last 10 mins to crisp bacon.

Beef and potato bake

Yield: 4 serves

Ingredients:

2 white onions finely sliced into rings

500g rump steak thinly sliced

Salt and pepper

2 large potatoes thinly sliced

1 cup milk

1 tbsp cornflour

Method:

1. Preheat oven to 180oC.
2. Layer the onion rings in the bottom of a casserole dish, then the beef slices and season with salt and pepper to taste.
3. Arrange potato slices on top and season again.
4. Mix together the milk and cornflour and pour over the top.
5. Bake for 1 hour.

Corned beef with parsley sauce

Yield: 4 serves

Ingredients:

1.5 kg corned silverside

2 dried bay leaves

6 black peppercorns

1 large brown onion quartered

1 large carrot chopped coarsely

1 tbsp brown malt vinegar

½ cup firmly packed brown sugar

PARSLEY SAUCE:

1 ½ tbsp butter

¼ cup plain flour

2 ½ cups milk

1/3 cup shredded tasty cheese

1/3 cup finely chopped fresh parsley

1 tbsp mild mustard

Method:

1. Place beef, bay leaves, peppercorns, onion, carrot, vinegar, and half the sugar in a large saucepan.
2. Add enough water to just cover the beef and let simmer covered for 2 hours or until beef is tender.
3. Cool beef for 1 hour in liquid in pan.
4. Remove beef from pan and discard the liquid.
5. Sprinkle sheet of foil with remaining sugar, wrap beef in foil and stand 20 mins then slice thinly.
6. Meanwhile make the parsley sauce.
7. Heat butter in small saucepan, dd flour, cook stirring until mixture thickens and bubbles.
8. Gradually stir in milk cook until sauce boils and thickens.
9. Remove from heat and stir in cheese, parsley and mustard.

10. Season to taste.
11. Serve sliced corned beef with parsley sauce.

Sausage bake

Yield: 4 serves

Ingredients:

6 thick sausages

2 cups chopped veggies (celery, onion, carrot, cauliflower)

½ cup shredded cheese

420g can condensed cream of mushroom soup

Method:

1. Preheat oven to 150Oc.
2. Combine all ingredients in a casserole dish and season with salt and pepper.
3. Bake covered for 45 mins at 150oC then uncover and cook for a further 15-20 mins.
4. You can serve this with crusty bread.

Easy beef stroganoff

Yield: 4 serves

Ingredients:

2 tbsp olive oil

500g beef stir fry strips

1 brown onion finely chopped

200g button mushrooms thinly sliced

175g packet beef stroganoff recipe base

2 tsp Italian herbs

2 tbsp sour cream

375g fettucine

2 tbsp chopped chives

Steamed carrots and steamed broccolini to serve

Method:

1. Heat half the oil in a large frying pan over medium-high heat.
2. Cook the beef in 2 batches for 3-4 mins or until lightly browned and transfer to a plate.
3. Heat the remaining oil in the pan over medium heat.
4. Cook the onion, stirring for 3-4 mins or until softened.
5. Add the mushroom and cook stirring for 2-3 mins or until mushroom is lightly browned.
6. Stir in the recipe base and herbs.
7. Bring to the boil and return the beef to the pan.
8. Reduce heat to low.
9. Bring to a simmer and cook stirring occasionally for 8-10 mins or until the beef is tender.
10. Add the sour cream and cook for 1 min or until heated through.
11. Meanwhile cook the pasta in a large saucepan of salted boiling water following packet directions.
12. Divide the pasta evenly among the bowls.

13. Top with the stroganoff and sprinkle with chives, season and serve with carrots and broccolini.

Mince rissoles

Yield: 4-5 serves

Ingredients:

1kg beef mince

4 tbsp bbq sauce

2 tbsp tomato sauce

1 egg

1 onion diced

Good couple of sprinkles of breadcrumbs

Method:

1. In a large bowl place, the beef mince and break up as best you can.
2. Add all other ingredients to the mince.
3. Get in with your hands and mix thoroughly to combine.
4. In a large frying pan spray with cooking oil.
5. Grab a handful of mixture and roll into a rissole and do the same with the rest of the rissole mixture.
6. Cook on a medium – high heat and turn every 5 mins until cooked takes about 20 mins.
7. Sometimes they do fall apart but still delicious to eat.
8. Serve with mashed potato.

SEAFOOD RECIPES

Salmon patties

Yield: 2-4 serves

Ingredients:

1 210ml tin of salmon

1 potato

½ onion

½ carrot

½ tsp salt

1 egg white

Breadcrumbs

Cooking spray

Method:

1. Chop onion thin, peel and chop up potato and boil together in some salty water.
2. Mash and cool.
3. Preheat oven to 180oC.
4. Grate carrot and add to salmon.
5. Once the potato mash is cool add it to the salmon and mix together with egg white.
6. Roll into patties then dip in breadcrumbs.
7. Place on a greased tray and bake in the oven for 20-25 mins.

Speedy salmon noodle stirfry

Yield: 4 serves

Ingredients:

270g packet soba noodles

400g skinless salmon fillets cut into 2cm pieces

2 carrots peeled and cut into long matchsticks

200g snow peas halved lengthways

175g packet kantong chicken and cashew nut stirfry sauce

Method:

1. Cook the noodles in a large saucepan of boiling water for 5 mins or until tender.
2. Drain well.
3. Meanwhile heat a greased wok or large frying pan over a high heat.
4. Stirfry half the salmon for 2-3 mins or until golden.
5. Transfer to a bowl.
6. Repeat with remaining salmon.
7. Add the carrot and snow peas to the wok or pan.
8. Stirfry for 1-2 mins or until just tender.
9. Return the salmon to the wok or pan with the noodles and stirfry sauce.
10. Stirfry for 1-2 mins or until heated through.
11. Divide noodle mixture among serving bowls.
12. Serve immediately.

Cherry tomato and roasted garlic prawn linguine

Yield: 4 serves

Ingredients:

375g dried linguine

50g butter chopped

700g medium green prawns, peeled and deveined tails intact

420g bottle sacla cherry tomato and roasted garlic pasta sauce

Fresh chopped parsley leaves to serve

Method:

1. Cook pasta in a large sauce pan of boiling water, following the packet instructions.
2. Drain and reserve ¼ cup of pasta water.
3. Meanwhile melt half the butter in a large deep-frying pan over a medium-high heat until foaming.
4. Add prawns and cook stirring occasionally for 2-3 mins or until just pink.
5. Add sauce and bring to a simmer.
6. Cook for 4-5 mins or until prawns are cooked through.
7. Add pasta, reserved pasta water and remaining butter to the pan.
8. Toss over low heat to combine.
9. Season with salt and pepper.
10. Serve sprinkled with parsley.

Garlic Prawns

Yield: 8 serves

Ingredients:

1/3 cup olive oil

20g butter

1 onion finely chopped

½ tsp chilli flakes

½ tsp fennel seeds

1kf raw banana prawns, peeled and deveined tails intact

4 garlic cloves finely chopped

1 tsp ground paprika

1 lemon zested finely grated and juiced

2 tbsp fresh parsley chopped

4 slices stone baked white sourdough toasted

Method:

1. Heat oil and butter in a large heavy frying pan over medium-high heat.
2. When butter has melted, add onion, chilli flakes and fennel seeds.
3. Cook stirring often for 2 mins or until onion softens.
4. Increase heat to medium -high and stir in the prawns, garlic and paprika.
5. Sprinkle with salt and pepper.
6. Cook stirring often for 3-4 mins or until prawns are cooked through.
7. Remove from heat and stir in lemon zest, 1 tbsp lemon juice and parsley.
8. Check seasoning and add more salt, pepper or lemon juice if necessary.
9. Spoon prawns and sauce onto serving plates and serve with bread toasted.

Homemade fish and chips

Yield: 4 serves

Ingredients:

½ cup breadcrumbs

1 tbsp parmesan cheese

1 egg

400g white fish (snapper, flathead, whiting) and cut into strips

2 large potatoes cut into chips

Cooking oil spray

Method:

1. Mix breadcrumbs and cheese together.
2. Whisk egg in a separate bowl.
3. Place fish in egg then add fish to breadcrumbs.
4. Completely cover fish with mixture.
5. Bbq on hot plate until cooked through.
6. Place potato sprayed with cooking oil on baking paper lined tray.
7. Cook at 200oC until chips are cooked.

Parmesan crumbed baked fish

Yield: 4 serves

Ingredients:

½ cup breadcrumbs

¼ cup flat leaf parsley leaves finely chopped

1/3 cup finely grated parmesan cheese

1 tsp finely grated lemon rind

4 thick white fish steaks

Olive oil cooking spray

Steamed green beans and boiled potatoes to serve

Method:

1. Preheat oven to 200oC.
2. Combine breadcrumbs, parsley, parmesan, lemon rind, salt and pepper in a bowl.
3. Stir to combine.
4. Drizzle with oil.
5. Stir until breadcrumbs are coated in oil.
6. Press breadcrumb mixture onto flesh side of fish fillets to form an even topping.
7. Place fish, skin down onto a baking tray.
8. Spray with oil.
9. Bake for 15 mins or until crumbs are light golden and fish is just cooked through.
10. Serve with steamed beans and potatoes.

LAMB RECIPES

Lamb pasties

Yield: 4 serves

Ingredients:

4 frozen puff pastry sheets, thawed

1 tbsp olive oil

1 onion finely chopped

350g lean lamb mince

1 tsp ground cinnamon

1 tsp ground cumin

¼ cup chopped mint leaves

2 tomatoes chopped

1 egg beaten to brush

Method:

1. Preheat oven to 190oC.
2. Cut four circles from the pastry sheet.
3. Transfer to a lined tray.
4. Chill while you make the filling.
5. Heat oil in a large frying pan over medium-high heat, then cook the onion, stirring for 1-2 mins until starts to soften.
6. Add mince and spices and cook, breaking up mince with a wooden spoon for 5-6 mins until meat is browned.
7. Season, add mint and tomato then remove from heat and cool.
8. Divide lamb among pastry, spooning it over half of each circle and leaving a 1cm border.
9. Brush edges with egg, then fold over to form parcels.
10. Press edges to seal, decorate with pastry off cuts if desired, then brush all over with egg.
11. Bake for 15 mins or until golden.
12. Cool.

Chutney lamb chops

Yield: 4 serves
Ingredients:
8 lamb chops
½ cup water
3 tsp curry powder
1 tbsp brown sugar
1 tsp soy sauce
½ cup fruit chutney
1 tsp mustard powder

Method:

1. Put water, curry powder, soy sauce, chutney, salt and pepper, mustard, and brown sugar into a bowl and mix well.
2. Place the chops into the slow cooker.
3. Pour the sauce over the top.
4. Cook on low for 6 hours.

Lamb cannelloni

Yield: 4 serves

Ingredients:

2 tsp olive oil

600g lean lamb mince

3 tsp Tuscan seasoning

700g bottle chunky tomato pasta sauce

100g feta, crumbled

250g packet fresh cannelloni sheets

¾ cup shredded mozzarella cheese

Method:

1. Heat oil in frying pan over medium-high heat.
2. Cook mince, stirring with a wooden spoon to break up mince for 6-8 mins or until browned and cooked through.
3. Add seasoning, stirring to combine.
4. Add ½ cup pasta sauce.
5. Cook stirring for 1-2 mins or until thick.
6. Transfer mixture to a bowl.
7. Stir in feta and season with pepper.
8. Preheat oven to 200oC.
9. Grease a rectangular baking dish.
10. Spoon ¼ cup remaining pasta sauce over the base of the prepared dish.
11. Place 1 cannelloni sheet on a board.
12. Spoon ¼ cup mince mixture along one long side.
13. Roll up to enclose filling.
14. Place seam side down in prepared dish and then repeat with the remaining cannelloni sheets and mixture.
15. Pour remaining pasta sauce over cannelloni and sprinkle with cheese.

16. Bake for 25-30 mins or until top is golden and cannelloni is tender then serve.

Roast lamb

Yield: 10 serves

Ingredients:

1 1/2kg lamb roast leg

1 splash olive oil

2 tbsp Capilano dark and bold honey

2 tbsp wholegrain mustard

4 sprigs fresh rosemary

Method:

1. Use a knife to make small cuts in the meat.
2. Rub oil into meat.
3. Mix mustard and honey together, then rub all over the meat or you can also baste, pressing into the cuts.
4. Insert sprigs of rosemary into the cuts.
5. Bake at 180oC for 2 hours.
6. Rest meat in aluminium foil for 15 mins before carving.

Lamb cutlets Kilpatrick

Yield: 4 serves
Ingredients:
16 lamb cutlets
6 slices of bacon, chopped
½ cup bbq sauce

Method:

1. In a large frying pan, cook the cutlets over a high heat for 2-3 mins of each side or until done to your liking.
2. Place on a paper lined tray and let rest.
3. Meanwhile, preheat the grill.
4. To the same pan, add chopped bacon and sauté until just cooked.
5. Season to taste.
6. Top each cutlet with the sticky bacon mixture and grill for 1-2 mins or until nice and crispy.

Moroccan lamb shanks

Yield: 6 serves

Ingredients:

1 tbsp olive oil

6 small lamb shanks french trimmed

1 brown onion finely chopped

2 carrots peeled and coarsely chopped

3 garlic cloves crushed

2 tsp ground cumin

1 tsp ground turmeric

1 tsp sweet paprika

1 x 7cm cinnamon stick

1L chicken stock

600g sweet potato peeled and coarsely chopped

1 x 400g can brown lentils rinsed and drained

100g pitted dried dates halved

Cooked couscous to serve

Fresh coriander leaves to serve

Method:

1. Heat the oil in a stockpot over a medium high heat and cook half the lamb turning occasionally for 4-5 mins or until browned.
2. Transfer to a plate and repeat with remaining lamb, reheating the pan between batches.
3. Add the onion, carrot and garlic to the pan.
4. Cook stirring for 5 mins then add the cumin, turmeric, paprika and cinnamon and cook stirring for 30 secs or until aromatic.
5. Stir in the stock and add the lamb and stir to coat.
6. Cover and bring to the boil, then reduce heat to low and let simmer for 1 hour.
7. Add sweet potato, lentils and dates then increase heat to high.
8. Cook uncovered for 30 mins or until lamb is tender.

9. Set aside for 10 mins to rest.
10. Season with salt and pepper.
11. Divide the couscous among the serving dishes.
12. Top with lamb and sauce then sprinkle with coriander and serve.

Poached lamb with spring vegetables

Yield: 4-6 serves

Ingredients:

2 cups beef stock

1 bag of baby carrots, diced

3 turnips, diced

8 potatoes peeled and diced

4 onions halved

1 bunch broccolini trimmed

1 cup broad beans trimmed

120g green beans trimmed

550g lamb back straps trimmed

Basil pesto to serve

Method:

1. Place stock in a large saucepan over a medium-high heat.
2. Season and bring to a simmer then add the carrots, turnips and potatoes.
3. Cook for 6-8 until tender.
4. Add the onions, broccolini, broad beans and green beans, then cook for a further 1-2 mins until tender.
5. Remove the vegetables with a slotted spoon and divide among serving bowls, mashing a little potato against the side of the pan using a fork to thicken the stock.
6. Thinly slice the lamb as thin as possible and divide among the bowls, pour over the hot stock (the stock will gently cook the lamb) drizzle with pesto and serve.

Mongolian lamb

Yield: 4 serves

Ingredients:

600g lamb steak

1 cup onion sliced

1 cup capsicum sliced

1 cup water

1 tsp crushed ginger

1 tsp crushed garlic

1 tbsp hoi sin sauce

2 tbsp soy sauce

1 tbsp oyster sauce

2 tsp sesame seeds

1 tsp beef stock powder

1 tsp sugar

2 tbsp cornflour

Cooking spray

Cooked rice or noodles to serve

Method:

1. Cut lamb into strips.
2. In a non-stick frying pan or wok with coated with cooking spray sauté the lamb, ginger and garlic until meat is nearly cooked.
3. Add onion and capsicum and cook for a further 2 mins.
4. Combine cornflour with water and add to the pan with all other remaining ingredients.
5. Bring to the boil and then serve with cooked rice or noodles.

Slow roasted lamb shanks with silverbeet

Yield: 4 serves

Ingredients:

8 frenched lamb shanks

2 tbsp olive oil

2 brown onions sliced

2 heads of garlic halved crossways

15g punnet of fresh thyme

10g fresh rosemary

3 cups dry white wine

1 lemon finely zested and juiced

3 bunches silverbeet leaves coarsely chopped

Method:

1. Preheat oven to 150oC and rub lamb with the oil and season with salt and pepper and divide the onions, garlic, thyme, rosemary between 2 baking dishes.
2. Place 4 lamb shanks in each dish and pour 1 ½ cups of wine in each dish and cover tightly with foil.
3. Roast in the oven for 3 hours or until lamb is completely tender and raise the oven temp to 250oC.
4. Remove the foil and turn lamb over and cook the lamb uncovered for until heavily caramelised.
5. Transfer the lamb to a plate.
6. Cover and set aside and strain the cooking liquid from the baking dishes into a measuring jug, reserving the onions and garlic.
7. Allow the fat to settle at the top and spoon off as much fat as possible.
8. Transfer the cooking liquid to a large heavy pot and stir in the lemon zest and juice and bring to a simmer over a medium heat.
9. Add the silverbeet and cook stirring for 3 mins or until wilted and season with salt and pepper.

10. Transfer the silverbeet to a platter and place the lamb, garlic and onion on top.

11. Spoon some of the pan juices from the silverbeet over the lamb and serve the remaining pan juice on the side.

PORK RECIPES

Honey glazed pork

Yield: 4 serves

Ingredients:

1/3 cup honey

¼ cup light soy sauce

3 garlic cloves crushed

1 tbsp sesame oil

4 pork cutlets

Steamed jasmine rice to serve

Method:

1. Combine honey, soy sauce, garlic and 2 tbsp water in a medium jug and set aside.
2. Heat oil in a large frying pan over a medium-high heat and add the pork.
3. Cook for 2-3 mins each side or until browned.
4. Add honey mixture and cook for a further 3 mins turning pork halfway or until glaze thickens and pork is cooked to your liking.
5. Serve with steamed rice.

Pork with crushed potatoes

Yield: 4 serves

Ingredients:

700g potatoes chopped

1 tbsp olive oil

8 pork loin chops

2 garlic cloves crushed

1 tbsp wholegrain mustard

½ cup chicken stock

100g baby spinach

Method:

1. Place potatoes into a saucepan and cover with cold water and add a pinch of salt.
2. Bring to the boil over a high heat.
3. Reduce heat to medium and cook for 12-15 mins or until tender.
4. Drain then set aside.
5. Heat oil in a non-stick frying pan over a medium-high heat.
6. Season both side of the pork with salt and pepper and cook for 2 mins on each side or until cooked to your liking.
7. Transfer to a plate and cover to keep warm.
8. Add potatoes, garlic and mustard to a hot frying pan.
9. Mash lightly with a potato masher so potatoes are just crushed then add stock and spinach and toss until spinach has wilted.
10. Serve pork with crushed potatoes.

Best ever meatloaf

Yield: 4 serves

Ingredients:

½ cup breadcrumbs

400g beef mince

300g pork mince

1 zucchini grated

1 carrot grated

1 egg lightly beaten

1 garlic clove crushed

2 tbsp bbq sauce

2 tbsp tomato sauce

Salt and pepper

1 tomato sliced

1/3 cup shredded cheddar cheese

Method:

1. Preheat oven to 200oC.
2. Place breadcrumbs, mince, zucchini, carrot, egg garlic, sauces, salt and pepper in a large bowl and mix well until combined.
3. Transfer mince mixture to a lightly greased loaf tin.
4. Bake for 25 mins top with tomato and cheese and then bake for another 15 mins.

Roast pork with apple gravy

Yield: 6 serves

Ingredients:

Olive oil to grease

3kg roast pork

¼ cup extra virgin olive oil

3 garlic cloves crushed

1 tbsp fresh rosemary leaves chopped

1 tsp salt

2 cups apple juice

2 tbsp plain flour

1 cup water

Method:

1. Brush a large roasting pan with oil to lightly grease.
2. Use a sharp knife to score the pork rind in a diamond pattern to the fat layer.
3. Combine the oil, garlic, rosemary and salt in a bowl.
4. Season with pepper and rub the oil mixture over the pork rind and flesh.
5. Transfer to the prepared pan.
6. Preheat oven to 200oC.
7. Add 250ml (1 cup) of apple juice to the roasting pan.
8. Roast in oven for 20 mins. Reduce oven temp to 180oC.
9. Roast for a further 2 hours or until cooked to your liking.
10. Transfer to a serving platter and cover with foil and set aside for 20 mins.
11. Meanwhile skim the surface of the pan juices to remove excess fat.
12. Tip the roasting pan containing juices into a saucepan and cook on a medium-low heat.
13. Add the flour and stir until well combined.

14. Stir in remaining apple juice and bring to the toil stirring continuously.
15. Cook for 2 mins or until mixture thickens.
16. Stir in water and bring to the boil.
17. Season with salt and pepper and strain into a heated serving jug.
18. Cut the pork and crackling into slices.
19. Serve with gravy.

Footy meatballs

Yield: depends on how big you make them

Ingredients:

650g pork mince

½ red onion finely chopped

¼ cup breadcrumbs

½ cup shredded tasty cheese

1 egg lightly beaten

2 garlic cloves crushed

2 fresh basil leaves finely chopped

1 tbsp parsley finely chopped

½ tsp dried oregano

1 tsp salt

1 tsp pepper

To serve choice of tomato sauce bbq sauce or sweet chilli sauce

Method:

1. Preheat oven to 180oC.
2. Line a tray with baking paper.
3. Place all ingredients in a large bowl and mix well with clean wet hands.
4. Roll mixture into small balls and place onto tray.
5. Bake for 30-40 mins until golden.
6. Serve with your choice of sauce.

Pork and apple meatballs

Yield: 4-6 serves

Ingredients:

500g pork mince

½ tsp ground fennel seeds

2 granny smith or green apples peeled and grated

1 egg

¼ cup breadcrumbs

Salt and pepper

1 ½ tbsp olive oil

Method:

1. Place all the ingredients except olive oil in a mixing bowl and use hands to combine well.
2. Roll the mixture into 30 balls and place on baking tray.
3. Refrigerate for an hour uncovered this firms them up.
4. Heat the oil in a frying pan over a medium heat and cook the meatballs for 12 mins carefully turning them every few mins so they are golden on all sides.

Bacon and egg pie

Yield: 4 serves

Ingredients:

Cooking spray

2 sheets puff pastry

500g bacon diced

1 onion finely diced

6 eggs

375ml evaporated milk

Salt and pepper

1 cup grated cheese

Method:

1. Preheat oven to 180oC.
2. Spray a baking dish with canola oil spray and line it with the pastry.
3. Overlap the pastry slightly and make sure it goes up at least 2 cm up the sides of the dish and has no holes.
4. Fry the bacon and onion until almost crispy.
5. Pour the mixture over the pastry and spread it evenly.
6. In a bowl whisk together the eggs and evaporated milk and season with salt and pepper.
7. Pour the mixture carefully into the dish.
8. Scatter the cheese on top and pop in the oven for approximately 30 mins or until set and golden on top.

Saucy pork chops

Yield: 4 serves

Ingredients:

4 pork chops

1 onion diced

1 cup tomato sauce

½ cup bbq sauce

½ cup brown sugar

Method:

1. Put the pork chops into the slow cooker and place onion on top.
2. In a bowl mix the sauces and brown sugar, then pour over the top of the pork chops.
3. Cover and cook on low for 3 hours.
4. Place a tea towel under the lid and cook for a further 1 hour.
5. Serve the chops with mashed potato and vegetables and spoon over the sauce over the pork chops before serving.

Cheese and bacon puffs

Yield: as many as you want depending on the size

Ingredients:

½ cup milk

2 cups shredded cheese

3 bacon rashers chopped

2 medium onions finely chopped

1 cup self-raising flour

1 tsp french mustard

310g canned corn optional

½ cup spring onions sliced

1 egg

1 pinch of salt and pepper to taste

Method:

1. Preheat oven to 180oC.
2. Combine cheese, bacon, onions, spring onions, corn, and flour in a large bowl.
3. Add the egg, milk and mustard and mix well.
4. Drop rounded tablespoons of mixture on oven trays line with baking paper.
5. They will spread slightly.
6. Bake for 20 mins.

Mini quiches

Yield: 24 serves

Ingredients:

5 large eggs

130ml cream

1 tbsp onion grated

2 ½ sheets puff pastry

1 cup shredded cheese

½ cup ham chopped

Method:

1. Preheat oven 210oC.
2. Grease muffin tray.
3. Using a fork, beat eggs, cream, onion, and salt and pepper in a bowl until well combined.
4. Cut and line each muffin hole with pastry.
5. Divide ham and cheese into muffin holes, and spoon in egg mixture.
6. Bake for 20-22 mins.

Potato and bacon bake

Yield: 4 serves

Ingredients:

7 washed potatoes sliced

3 onions sliced

250g bacon diced

1 packet french onion soup mix

250ml thickened cream

Tasty cheese to taste

Method:

1. Preheat oven to 180oC.
2. Layer potatoes, onion and bacon in a casserole dish.
3. Mix together the soup mix and cream.
4. Pour over the top of everything.
5. Bake in oven for 45 mins or until potato is cooked.
6. Sprinkle with shredded cheese and serve.

Egg and bacon pizza

Yield: 4 serves

Ingredients:

4 bacon rashers

4 wraps

4 tbsp sundried tomato pesto

100g shredded mozzarella

4 eggs

12 cherry tomatoes optional

Olive oil optional

Method:

1. Preheat oven to 200oC.
2. Cut each rasher into 3 slices.
3. Line a baking tray with baking paper and spread bacon out in a single layer.
4. Cook in oven for 5-7 mins or until just starting to crisp.
5. Replace baking paper with a fresh sheet.
6. Place pizza/wrap bases on the baking paper and spread with sundried tomato pesto.
7. Lay 3 pieces of bacon around the edge of each pizza and sprinkle cheese over the top of the bacon.
8. Carefully break an egg into the centre of each pizza.
9. Drizzle each pizza with olive oil (optional).
10. Season with salt and pepper and bake for 8-10 mins or until egg has just cooked and the tomatoes (optional) have started to wilt.

PASTA RECIPES

My carbonara

Yield: 4-6 serves

Ingredients:

400g bacon pieces

2 tins carnation milk

1 cup shredded cheese

2-3 tbsp parmesan cheese

2 onions diced

4 garlic cloves minced

Macaroni pasta

Method:

1. Bring to the boil a medium pot of salted water and cook pasta as per packet instructions.
2. In a fry pan fry bacon pieces, garlic and onion until a nice colour forms or until your satisfied with it.
3. Place carnation milk in the fry pan on top of bacon, garlic and onion and stir through until warmed up.
4. Add in cheese and stir through until melted.
5. Let simmer but keep stirring every few mins.
6. Once pasta is cooked, drain and put into bowls then spoon sauce of the top and serve.

Macaroni pasta bake

Yield: 4-6 serves

Ingredients:

2 cups cooked macaroni pasta

420g can condensed tomato soup

250g diced ham

1 cup shredded cheese

Method:

1. Preheat oven to 200oC.
2. Lightly grease an ovenproof dish.
3. Place pasta in the dish.
4. In a separate bowl mix soup and ham together.
5. Pour over the top and stir through the pasta.
6. Sprinkle cheese over the top.
7. Place in oven for 20-30 mins or until cheese is melted and golden.

Frugal pasta

Yield: 4-6 serves

Ingredients:

Any type of pasta

Butter

Method:

1. Cook the pasta as per packet instructions.
2. Drain and mix in a few tbsp butter.
3. Serve.

Tuscan style pasta

Yield: 4-6 serves
Ingredients:
500g fettucine
4 tins whole tomatoes
250g butter softened
4 onions peeled and quartered

Method:

1. Fill a large pot with salted water and bring to the boil.
2. Add the fettucine and cook as per packet instructions.
3. Remove and drain.
4. Rinse the pot and put it back on the stove on a medium-high heat.
5. Add tomatoes, butter and onions and bring it to the boil.
6. Reduce the heat and simmer for 2 hours, allowing time for the delicious flavours to develop.

Simple spaghetti

Yield: 4-6 serves

Ingredients:

1 packet penne pasta

2 tbsp butter

1 cup cheddar cheese

1 cup tomato sauce

Method:

1. Cook pasta as per packet instructions.
2. Drain then place in saucepan.
3. Add butter mixing until melted.
4. Add tomato sauce and cheese and mix until cheese starts to melt.
5. Serve.

Ricotta and spinach gnocchi bake

Yield: 4 serves

Ingredients:

500g packet potato gnocchi

120g packet baby spinach

785g jar tomato, onion and garlic pasta sauce

200g firm ricotta

2/3 cup shredded pizza cheese

Method:

1. Cook gnocchi in a large saucepan of boiling water following packet instructions and then drain.
2. Return to the pan and add 2/3 of the spinach and half the pasta sauce and toss to combine.
3. Preheat grill on high.
4. Spread the remaining pasta sauce over the base of a baking dish.
5. Top with gnocchi mixture.
6. Crumble ricotta and sprinkle with pizza cheese and season.
7. Cook under grill for 5-6 mins or until cheese is golden and the gnocchi is heated through.
8. Serve with remaining spinach.

Pizza casserole

Yield: 2 serves

Ingredients:

2 cups uncooked egg noodles

250g beef mince

1 onion chopped

2 garlic cloves minced

1 green capsicum

1 cup pepperoni sliced

500ml pizza sauce

4 tbsp milk

1 cup shredded mozzarella cheese

Method:

1. Cook noodles according to package directions.
2. Preheat oven to 175oC.
3. In a medium pan over medium-high heat brown mince beef with onion, garlic and capsicum.
4. Drain excess fat.
5. Stir in noodles, pepperoni, pizza sauce and milk and mix well.
6. Transfer to a casserole dish.
7. Bake for 20 mins remove from the oven top with cheese and bake for 5-10 mins until cheese is melted.

Pasta with meatballs

Yield: 4 serves
Ingredients:
2 420g packet beef meatballs
400g penne
190g jar tomato pesto
125g feta crumbled
100g baby rocket to serve

Method:

1. Heat a large frying pan and cook meatballs over a medium-high heat for 10 mins, turning often until well browned and cooked through.
2. Meanwhile cook the pasta as per packet instructions.
3. Drain and return to the pan.
4. Add pesto and toss to combine.
5. Serve tossed with meatballs and top with feta and rocket leaves.

15-minute carbonara pasta

Yield: 4 serves

Ingredients:

375g spaghetti

1 tbsp olive oil

200g shortcut bacon rashers cut into 2 cm long pieces

2 eggs

2 egg yolks

½ cup pure cream

2/3 cup parmesan cheese finely grated

Fresh Parsley leaves

Method:

1. Cook pasta in a large saucepan of boiling salted water, following packet directions until tender.
2. Drain and return to pan.
3. Meanwhile heat oil in a frying pan over medium-high heat.
4. Add bacon and cook for 4 mins or until crisp.
5. Whisk eggs, egg yolks, cream and parmesan in a jug and season with pepper.
6. Add bacon and egg mixture to pasta.
7. Cook tossing over low heat for 1 min or until combined and top with parsley.

Spaghetti with creamy ham sauce

Yield: 6 serves

Ingredients:

500g spaghetti

Spray oil for cooking

1 small onion finely diced

150g button mushrooms diced (optional)

2 garlic cloves crushed

1 tbsp cornflour

375ml tin carnation milk

200g ham cut into strips

1 tbsp chopped parsley

Method:

1. Cook pasta according to packet directions.
2. Drain and keep warm.
3. Meanwhile heat frying pan over medium-high heat and spray with oil.
4. Add onion and mushrooms and cook for 3 mins or until soft.
5. Add garlic and cook for 1 min.
6. Blend cornflour with ¼ cup carnation milk.
7. Add to the frying pan with remaining carnation milk, stirring constantly until the sauce boils and thickens.
8. Stir in ham and parsley and season to taste.
9. Add pasta and cook just until heated through.

Bacon and broccoli pasta

Yield: 2-4 serves

Ingredients:

375g pasta

1 head broccoli cut into small pieces

¾ cup peas

1 cup beans

3 rashers bacon thickly sliced

Method:

1. Fill a large pot with water and bring to the boil.
2. Add pasta packet of your favourite pasta ad follow the cooking time on the packet.
3. Drain well and set aside.
4. Meanwhile using a steamer cook broccoli, peas and beans and then add to cooked pasta.
5. In a frying pan on a medium heat add a teaspoon of olive oil then toss the rashers of bacon in and cook until crispy.
6. Remove bacon from pan and place on paper towel to drain excess oil.
7. Add all of the ingredients to the pasta and mis together using tongs and serve.

SOUP RECIPES

Broccoli and sweet potato soup

Yield: 4 serves

Ingredients:

1 brown onion diced

500g broccoli stems finely chopped

500g sweet potato peeled and finely chopped

4 cups vegetable stock

½ cup Greek style yoghurt

Method:

1. Heat a medium saucepan over medium heat.
2. Add the onion, broccoli stems and sweet potato and cook, stirring often for 5 mins or until onion softens.
3. Add the stock and 2 cups of water and bring to the boil.
4. Reduce heat to low and add broccoli florets.
5. Cook for 15 mins or until sweet potato is tender.
6. Set aside to cool slightly.
7. Use a stick blender to carefully blend the soup until smooth.
8. Divide amongst the bowls and place yoghurt in a small bowl and stir in 2 tbsp of water.
9. Add to the soup and gently swirl and then season.

Carrot and coriander soup

Yield: 4-6 serves

Ingredients:

1.5L vegetable stock

2 large onions chopped

10 stems fresh coriander

8 large carrots roughly chopped

Method:

1. In a large saucepan heat the stock.
2. Add all other ingredients and bring to a gentle boil.
3. Reduce the heat to a simmer until the carrots are tender.
4. Season with cracked pepper.
5. Blend and serve.

Twisted pumpkin soup

Yield: 4-6 serves

Ingredients:

¾ medium butternut pumpkin skin and seeds removed and chopped

2 medium-large potatoes chopped

1 onion chopped

1 ½ tsp curry powder

Salt and pepper to taste

2 ½ cups vegetable stock

1 cup cream

Chilli powder to taste optional

Method:

1. Place pumpkin, potatoes, onion, curry powder and stock in a large slow cooker.
2. Season with salt and pepper.
3. Cook on low for 6 hours until vegetables are tender.
4. Turn off the slow cooker and allow to cool.
5. Using a food processor or stick blender process until smooth and then stir through the cream.
6. Warm the soup again in a saucepan or in the microwave, season to taste and then serve.

Cauliflower and bacon soup

Yield: 4-6 serves

Ingredients:

400g cauliflower cut into florets

150g bacon roughly chopped

2 tbsp lemon juice

1 cup chicken stock

Method:

1. In a large saucepan sauté the bacon until just golden.
2. Add the cauliflower and toss together for 2 mins.
3. Season with cracked pepper.
4. Add lemon juice and stock.
5. Simmer until the cauliflower is tender about 15-20 mins.
6. Remove from heat and allow to cool then puree until smooth.

Vegetable weight loss soup

Yield: 6-8 serves

Ingredients:

2 zucchinis grated

2 carrots grated

1 red capsicum diced

1 green capsicum diced

2 tins diced tomatoes

2-3 tbsp minced garlic

1L vegetable stock

½ cabbage diced

1 brown onion diced

Any other vegetables you want to put in

Method:

1. Combine all ingredients in a large slow cooker and cook on low for 6-8 hours.
2. Once cooked you can also blend together using a stick blender.

Pea and ham soup

Yield: 4 serves
Ingredients:
3 carrots
½ parsnip
1 onion
300g peas
300g ham hock
1 ½ tsp salt
5 cups water

Method:

1. Peel and dice the carrots and parsnip.
2. Peel and finely dice the onion.
3. Place in the slow cooker with the remaining ingredients and stir.
4. Cook on high for 4 hours or on low for 8 hours.

Leek and potato soup

Yield: 6 serves

Ingredients:

1kg leeks

600g potatoes

2 cups chicken stock

¾ cup evaporated milk

½ cup shredded tasty cheese

White pepper to serve

Method:

1. Remove the green section of the leeks and discard them.
2. Wash the white section of the leeks well and cut into 1 cm piece.
3. Place in the slow cooker.
4. Peel the potatoes and cut into 1 cm pieces.
5. Add to the slow cooker with the chicken stock.
6. Cook on high for 4 hours or 8 hours on low.
7. Puree with a stick blender.
8. Turn off the heat and then add the cream and cheese and stir to combine.
9. Add salt and white pepper to taste.

Hearty lamb and vegetable soup

Yield: 6 serves

Ingredients:

125g sweet potato

2 carrots

1 onion

2 lamb shanks

2 tbsp peas

1 tsp salt

4 cups water

Method:

1. Peel and dice the sweet potato, carrots and onion.
2. Place in the slow cooker with remaining ingredients and stir.
3. Cook on high for 4 hours or low or 8 hours.
4. Season with salt and pepper to serve.

Chicken soup

Yield: 4-6 serves

Ingredients:

2 chicken fillets diced

2 carrots peeled and shred

1 parsnip peel and shred

1 turnip shredded

1 large onion diced

2 sticks of celery diced

2 packets of chicken soup

½ pot of water

Method:

1. Place all ingredients in a large pot and bring to the boil and then simmer for 1 ½ hours until cooked.

Curried zucchini soup

Yield: 4 serves

Ingredients:

1 onion

1 ½ tbsp butter

2 tsp curry powder

1 garlic clove crushed

500g zucchini

1 tbsp lemon juice

Salt and pepper

2 ½ cups chicken stock

2/3 cup cream

Method:

1. Coarsely chop onion.
2. Melt butter in a pan then add onion, curry powder and crushed garlic.
3. Cook stirring for a few mins or until onion is transparent.
4. Place mixture into blender with roughly chopped zucchini, lemon juice and about half the stock.
5. Blend until vegetables are finely chopped.
6. Stir in remaining stock and cream.
7. Cover and refrigerate for a few hours.
8. Push through a fine strainer and discard vegetable pulp.
9. Season with salt and pepper.
10. You can warm up in the microwave too.

Roasted sweet potato and carrot soup

Yield: 4 serves

Ingredients:

500g sweet potato peeled and cut into chunks

300g carrots peeled and cut into chunks

3 tbsp olive oil

2 onions finely chopped

2 garlic cloves crushed

1L vegetable stock

100ml crème fraiche plus extra to serve

Method:

1. Preheat oven to 220oC.
2. Put sweet potato and carrots in a roasting tray and drizzle with 2 tbsp and plenty of seasoning.
3. Roast the vegetables in the oven for 25-30 mins or until caramelised and tender.
4. Meanwhile put the remaining 1 tbsp olive oil in a large deep saucepan and fry the 2 onions over a medium-low heat for about 10 mins until softened.
5. Add garlic and stir for 1 min before adding 1L vegetable stock.
6. Simmer for 5-10 mins until the onions are very soft then set aside.
7. Once the roasted vegetables are done, leave to cool a little, then transfer to the saucepan and use a hand blender to process until smooth.
8. Stir in 100ml crème fraiche, a little more seasoning and reheat until hot.
9. Serve in bowls topped with a swirl of crème fraiche and a good grinding of black pepper.

Butternut pumpkin soup

Yield: 6 serves

Ingredients:

4 cups chicken stock

4 cups butternut pumpkin cubed

3 large carrots chopped

1 small onion diced

5 stalks celery diced

1 garlic clove minced

1 tsp curry powder

¼ tsp ginger

¼ tsp cinnamon

1 tin evaporated milk

Olive oil

Salt

Pepper

Method:

1. Preheat oven to 220oC.
2. Arrange pumpkin and carrots on a baking tray and drizzle with olive oil and sprinkle with salt and pepper.
3. Roast in oven for 20 mins.
4. In the meantime, drizzle olive oil in a large stockpot over medium heat.
5. Sauté onion, celery and garlic for 5 mins.
6. Add in spices and cook for 2 mins longer.
7. Remove from heat.
8. When pumpkin and carrots are finished, add to the pot.
9. Add chicken stock and cook and cover with lid over low heat for 20 mins.
10. Work in batches running soup through a blender until smooth.
11. Serve with a dollop of Greek yoghurt.

CAKES, DESSERTS AND YUMMY TREATS

Easy pantry staples cake

Yield: 8-10 slices

Ingredients:

1 cup self-raising flour

1 cup coconut

½ cup caster sugar

1 cup of milk

Method:

1. Preheat oven to 180oC.
2. Mix all ingredients together until well combined.
3. Grease and line a cake tin with baking paper.
4. Pour in mixture and cook for 40—45mins.
5. Nice served warm with cream or ice cream.

Banana ice cream

Yield: 4 serves

Ingredients:

4 ripe bananas, chopped

Method:

1. Freeze the bananas.
2. Place half in a blender with tbsp of water.
3. Blend for 30 secs then scrape down the sides.
4. Add half of the remaining bananas and blend for another 30 secs.
5. Again, scrape down the sides before adding final amount.
6. Blend now for 1-2 mins or until bananas turn into a rich creamy ice cream.

Chocolate rough slice

Yield: 24 slices

Ingredients:

Base:

1 cup self-raising flour

1 tbsp cocoa

1/3 cup caster sugar

Pinch of salt

¼ cup desiccated coconut

110g butter melted

Topping:

200g condensed milk

2 tbsp cocoa

1 cup icing sugar

1 ½ tbsp butter melted

1 cup desiccated coconut

1 tsp vanilla essence

Method:

1. Preheat oven to 180oC.
2. Grease and line a loaf tin with baking paper.
3. In a large bowl sift flour and cocoa, add salt, sugar, coconut and butter and mix to combine.
4. Press base mixture into the prepared slice tin.
5. Bake base for 20 mins or until golden and cooked through.
6. Rest on tray for 5 mins before transferring to a wire rack.
7. Make topping by combining all topping ingredients in a bowl and mix to combine.
8. Spread topping over the warm base and leave on wire rack to cool completely.

Fairy cakes

Yield: 12-24 cupcakes
Ingredients:
125g softened butter
2/3 cup caster sugar
2 eggs
1 cup plain flour
2 tsp baking powder
1 ½ tbsp milk

Method:

1. Preheat oven to 190oC.
2. Lay out 24 patty pans on a baking tray or cupcake tray if you have it.
3. Cream butter and sugar until light and fluffy.
4. Add eggs one at a time, beating well after each addition.
5. Sift flour and baking powder into mixture and add milk.
6. Mix thoroughly but do not beat.
7. Place a large tsp of mixture into each patty pan.
8. Bake for 15-20 mins or until cooked.
9. Allow to cool before decorating or icing.

Chocolate mousse

Yield: 6 serves

Ingredients:

300g dark chocolate roughly chopped

3 eggs at room temp

¼ cup caster sugar

1 tbsp cocoa powder sifted

300ml thickened cream plus extra whipped cream

Method:

1. Place the chocolate in a heatproof bowl over a pan of gently simmering water don't let the bowl touch the water.
2. Stir until melted.
3. Remove bowl from heat and set aside to cool slightly.
4. Place eggs and sugar in a large bowl and beat with electric beater for 5 mins or until mixture becomes pale, thick and doubled in size.
5. Fold in cocoa powder and cooled chocolate until combined.
6. In a separate bowl, whip cream until thickened be careful not to over beat.
7. Use a large metal spoon to carefully fold the cream into the chocolate mixture, trying to keep the mixture as light as possible.
8. Spoon into 6 serving glasses and chill in fridge for at least 1 hour.
9. Remove from fridge 15 mins before serving, then top with whipped cream and grated chocolate to serve.

Jelly slice

Yield: about 20 pieces
3 packets of jelly any flavour you like
3 cups boiling water
1 tbsp gelatine
1 cup of cream

Method:

1. Combine jelly, water and gelatine.
2. Stir until dissolved.
3. Add cream and stir through.
4. Pour into a slice tray and refrigerate overnight.
5. Cut into slices before serving.

Blueberry banana bread

Yield: 10 serves

Ingredients:

1 ¾ cups plain flour

1 tsp baking powder

1/8 tsp bicarb soda

½ cup butter softened

1 cup sugar

2 eggs

¼ cup milk

1 tsp vanilla

3 ripe bananas mashed

1 ¼ cup blueberries

Method:

1. Preheat oven to 175oC.
2. Prepare a loaf tin with cooking spray.
3. Combine flour, baking powder, bicarb soda, and salt and set aside.
4. In a separate bowl beat butter and sugar using an electric beater until light and fluffy.
5. Add eggs, milk and vanilla.
6. Mix until well combined.
7. Beat in bananas with the mixer at a low speed then gradually add in flour mixture until just combined.
8. Using a spatula fold in the blueberries.
9. Pour batter into the loaf tin.
10. Bake for 55-60 mins until skewer or knife comes out clean.
11. If it's getting too brown on top and not cooked place foil over the top and continue cooking.
12. Remove from the oven and let cool for 15 mins before removing from the pan.

Chocolate crackles

Yield: 16-24 depending on patty pan size

Ingredients:

3 cups of coco pops

1 200g block of dairy milk chocolate or cooking chocolate

150g buttered softened

Method:

1. Melt chocolate and butter over a low heat in a saucepan stir continuously to make sure it doesn't burn.
2. Once all melted take off heat and allow to cool.
3. Once cooled mix in coco pops and stir to combine, make sure all coco pops are covered in chocolate.
4. Spoon into patty pans and place into the fridge for a few hours or overnight.

Chocolate balls

Yield: as many as you want to make depends on size of the balls.

Ingredients:

250g packet marie biscuits crushed

3 tbsp cocoa

400g tin condensed milk

½ cup desiccated coconut

Method:

1. Mix crushed biscuits, cocoa and condensed milk together to make a sticky mix.
2. Using a tsp of mixture roll into balls and cover in coconut.
3. Put in a container and in the fridge to harden once all balls are made.

Anzac biscuits

Yield: depends on how big you make them

Ingredients:

1 ¼ cups plain flour sifted

1 cup rolled oats

½ cup caster sugar

¾ cup desiccated coconut

220g butter chopped

2 tbsp golden syrup

1 ½ tbsp water

½ tsp bicarb soda

Method:

1. Preheat oven to 170oC.
2. Place the flour, oats, sugar and coconut in a large bowl and stir to combine.
3. In a small saucepan place the golden syrup and butter and stir over low heat until butter has fully melted.
4. Mix the bicarb soda with 1 ½ tbsp water and add to the golden syrup mixture.
5. It will bubble while you stir together so remove from the heat.
6. Pour into the dry ingredients and mix together until fully combined.
7. Roll tablespoonfuls of mixture into balls and place on baking tray that's lined with baking paper, pressing down on top to flatten slightly.
8. Bake for 12 mins or until golden.

Chocolate pavlova

Yield: 6 serves

Ingredients:

1 ½ cup caster sugar

6 eggs whites

2 tbsp cocoa powder

500g strawberries

300ml double cream

Method:

1. Preheat oven to 120oC.
2. Line a baking tray with baking paper.
3. Reserve 2 tsp of the sugar.
4. Use and electric mixer to whisk the egg whites in a clean dry bowl until stiff peaks form.
5. Gradually add the remaining sugar, 1 tbsp at a time, whisking well after each addition.
6. Continue whisking for 5 mins or until sugar dissolves.
7. Sift cocoa powder over the meringue mixture.
8. Use a large metal spoon to gently fold to create a swirled effect.
9. Spoon onto the lined tray
10. Shape into 20 cm diameter domes.
11. Bake for 1 hour or until meringue is dry to touch.
12. Cool in oven with door ajar for 1 hour or until completely cool.
13. Meanwhile slice strawberries, leaving some whole.
14. Combine with reserved sugar in a medium bowl.
15. Set aside for 10 mins or until juices are released.
16. Carefully transfer the pavlova to a serving plate.
17. Top with cream and strawberry mixture.

Peppermint chocolate slice

Yield: about 20 pieces

Ingredients:

1 packet dark chocolate melts

3 drops peppermint essence

½ packet white chocolate melts

4 drops green food colouring

Method:

1. Line a square cake tin with baking paper.
2. Melt dark chocolate in a lightly heated saucepan stirring through-out until melted.
3. Add peppermint essence and stir.
4. Spread half the mixture evenly over the bottom of the tin and set it in fridge for 5 mins.
5. Melt white chocolate the same way then stir in green food colouring.
6. Spread this over the layer of the dark chocolate and then refriger-ate until set.
7. Spread remaining dark chocolate over the green/white chocolate and set in fridge.
8. Cut into pieces and store in fridge.

M&M bars

Yield: 16 bars
Ingredients:
220g arrowroot biscuits
400g tin condensed milk
1 cup of m&ms

Method:

1. Preheat oven to 160oC.
2. Line a baking tray with baking paper.
3. In a food processor or blender process biscuits until fine.
4. Pour into a large bowl and add the m&ms and condensed milk and stir well to combine.
5. Scrape the mixture into the tray and bake for 15-20 mins or until just golden.
6. Cool completely before serving.

Banana and sultana muffins

Yield: 10 serves

Ingredients:

2 cups wholemeal self-raising flour

¼ cup sugar

2 egg whites

1 ½ cups mashed bananas

½ cup sultanas

¾ tsp bicarb soda

½ cup apple sauce

Method:

1. Preheat oven to 200oC.
2. Beat egg whites and sugar for 1 min.
3. Stir in bananas.
4. In a separate bowl mix bicarb soda to the apple sauce then add to the bowl.
5. Gently fold in flour and sultanas until well combined.
6. Put in patty pans on a muffin tray and bake for 20 mins.

Homemade Kingston biscuits

Yield: about 30

Ingredients:

1 cup plain flour

¾ cup sugar

¼ tsp salt

1 ¼ cups quick oats

2/3 cup desiccated coconut

¼ cup golden syrup

115g butter

1 tsp bicarb soda

1 ½ tbsp boiling water

1 cup milk chocolate chips

Method:

1. Preheat oven to 160oC.
2. In a large bowl whisk together flour, sugar, oats, coconut and salt until well combined and set aside.
3. Combine golden syrup and butter in a small saucepan and melt together over a low heat.
4. Mix the bicarb soda with boiling water and add to the butter mixture.
5. It should start to get frothy straight away.
6. Mix in the dry ingredients with the wet ingredients.
7. Use about 2 tsp worth of cookie dough onto baking trays at least 5cm apart as they will spread.
8. Press down on top of each one to flatten it just slightly.
9. Bake for 12-14 mins turning the tray at the halfway mark.
10. Once cooled melt the chocolate in 20 second bursts in the microwave stirring well between each until JUST melted.

11. Let the chocolate cool to a consistency where it doesn't immediately flatten out when drizzled, then add ½ - 1 tsp to a cookie and then sandwich it together with another.
12. Let them set at room temp.

Jam sugar buns

Yield: 16 serves
Ingredients:
1 ½ cups self-raising flour
¼ tsp salt
¼ cup sugar
3 tbsp butter
1 egg
1/3 cup milk
½ tsp vanilla
Jam
Extra sugar for sprinkling
Cooking spray

Method:

1. Preheat oven to 180oC.
2. Sift flour and salt into a bowl and then add sugar.
3. Rub butter into dry ingredients.
4. Beat together egg, milk and vanilla.
5. Pour over dry mixture and mix to a stiff dough.
6. Drop spoonful's onto a tray lined with baking paper.
7. Make a finer mark by pushing down on the dough to make a hole.
8. Place ½ tsp of jam onto each one and close the hole.
9. Sprinkle with sugar and bake in the oven for 10-15 mins.

Madeira cake

Yield: 6-8 serves

Ingredients:

125g butter softened

1 cup caster sugar

2 eggs

1 tsp vanilla extract

1 ½ cups self-raising flour

½ cup milk

Method:

1. Preheat oven to 180oC.
2. Line a loaf tin with baking paper.
3. In a bowl, using a mixer cream the butter and sugar and add the vanilla.
4. Add the eggs one at a time mixing well with the milk.
5. Add flour and mix for 2 mins.
6. Pour into the loaf tin and bake for 50-55 mins.

Vanilla slice

Yield: 8 serves

Ingredients:

200g packet lattice biscuits

600ml cream

100g packet vanilla pudding mix

Passionfruit icing:

1 cup icing sugar

2 passionfruit pulp

1 tbsp butter softened

Method:

1. Line a 20 x 30cm dish with baking paper.
2. Layer with 8 lattice biscuits flat side up.
3. In a bowl, using electric beaters, mix cream and pudding until thick.
4. Spoon the creamy mixture over the biscuit base.
5. Top with another layer of biscuits, shiny side up.
6. Refrigerate for at least 30 mins before topping with passionfruit icing.
7. To make the icing, mix together the icing sugar, passionfruit and butter until an even spreadable consistency is reached.
8. Add more passionfruit if required.

Orange banana muffins

Yield: 12 serves

Ingredients:

1 coles packet butter or vanilla cake mix

2 oranges juiced

3 very ripe bananas

Method:

1. Preheat oven to 180oC.
2. In a mixing bowl pour in cake mix.
3. In a separate bowl mash, the bananas.
4. Add bananas to the cake mix and stir through.
5. Add in the 2 juiced oranges and stir through so it becomes a thick cupcake consistency.
6. In a muffin tray line with patty pans and add 1-1 ½ tbsp mixture to each.
7. Bake in the oven for 15 mins then turn it around while still in oven and cook for another 5 mins.

Scones

Yield: depending on the size you make them

Ingredients:

2 cups self-raising flour

¼ tsp salt

1 tbsp butter

¾ cup milk

Cooking spray

Method:

1. Grease tray and preheat oven to 230oC.
2. Sift flour and rub in butter with fingertips.
3. Add milk and mix to a soft dough.
4. Turn onto a lightly floured board and knead until smooth with floured fingers.
5. Roll out dough until 1.5 cm thick.
6. Cut into shapes with glass and place on tray and glaze the top with milk.
7. Bake for 7-10 mins.

Honey joys

Yield: about 12 depending on size, you make them

Ingredients:

1/3 cup butter

¼ cup sugar

2 tbsp honey

4 cups cornflakes

Patty pans

Method:

1. Preheat oven to 180oC.
2. Melt butter, sugar and honey in saucepan or in the microwave until dissolves.
3. Pour on cornflakes in a bowl and mix gently.
4. Put in patty pans and cook for 10 mins.

Chocolate chip muffins

Yield: 10 serves

Ingredients:

2 cups self-raising flour

2 egg whites

½ cup sugar

½ cup chocolate chips

½ cup apple sauce

½ cup milk

1 tsp vanilla essence

¾ tsp bicarb soda

Method:

1. Preheat oven to 200oC.
2. Beat eggs, sugar and essence for 1 mins.
3. Stir in bicarb and apple sauce in a separate bowl it will froth.
4. Then add to the egg mixture.
5. Gently fold in flour and choc chips alternating with milk until combined.
6. Add to patty pans in a muffin tray and bake for 20 mins.

Snow cakes

Yield: 12 serves

Ingredients:

1 coles vanilla cake mix

250ml lemonade

ICING:

½ cup of butter or 8 tbsp

1 ½ cups icing sugar

1 tsp vanilla essence

1 tbsp cocoa powder I just roughly sprinkled

Method:

1. Preheat your pie maker.
2. In a bowl mix together lemonade and cake mix until nick and thick.
3. In a little measuring cup get ¼ cup scoops of mixture and place into pie maker.
4. I had 4 spots on mine.
5. Once all spots have the mixture in it and close the lid and set a timer for 7 mins.
6. Once cooked take out the cakes of the pie maker and place on a cooling rack.
7. Repeat above step until all snow cakes have been made and have cooled.
8. Once cooled cut the tops off each of the snow cakes.
9. Make the icing except don't add the cocoa just yet and mix with an electric beater.
10. In a separate bowl take out 1/3 of the icing mixture and then add the cocoa powder to it and beat again until combined.
11. Using the vanilla icing spread of the middle of the cakes and then place lids back on top and cover with the chocolate icing.
12. Then the fun begins its time to eat.

Wicked chocolate cake

Yield: 6-8 serves

Ingredients:

1 ¼ cup self-raising flour

¼ cup cocoa

½ tsp bicarb soda

2 egg whites

¾ cup caster sugar

4 level tbsp margarine

¾ cup boiled water

ICING:

¾ cup icing sugar

1 level tbsp cocoa powder

1 ½ level tbsp milk

Method:

1. Preheat oven to 180oC.
2. Dissolve sugar and margarine in boiling water.
3. Sift flour, bicarb, and cocoa powder.
4. Using an electric beater for 1 min to combine.
5. Add eggs and beat for 30 seconds.
6. Pour into a lined and greased cake tin.
7. Cook for 30 mins.
8. When cake is cool mix icing together and place on top of cake.

Moist banana muffins

Yield: 6 serves

Ingredients:

¾ cup plain flour

2 ripe bananas mashed

1/8 cup olive oil

1/3 cup sugar

½ tsp vanilla essence

½ tsp bicarb soda

¾ tsp salt

½ tsp ground cinnamon

Method:

1. Preheat oven to 180oC.
2. Sift all the dry ingredients together and mix well.
3. In a separate bowl, combine mashed bananas with olive oil and vanilla essence.
4. Combine the dry ingredients with the banana mixture and mix well.
5. Pour mixture into muffin tray lined with patty pans until full.
6. Bake for 15-20 or until a toothpick comes out clean.

M&M chocolate chip cookies

Yield: 30 cookies

Ingredients:

125g western star butter

½ cup caster sugar

½ cup brown sugar

½ tsp brown sugar

½ tsp vanilla extract

1 lightly beaten egg

1 ¾ cup self-raising flour

½ tsp salt

¾ cup dark chocolate chips

¾ cup M&Ms

Method:

1. Preheat oven to 180oC and line some baking trays with baking paper and spray with olive oil.
2. Beat together butter, sugars, and vanilla until pale.
3. Add egg and beat some more until it is well combined.
4. Sift in flour and salt and mix well with a wooden spoon.
5. Then using clean hands mix the dough and squish it until it all comes together.
6. Add in chocolate chips and m&ms and mix in using your hands this gets the best distribution.
7. Shape the dough into small balls and place on prepared trays.
8. Make sure they have room to spread.
9. Bake for 10-12 mins.
10. Allow to cool for 5 mins after you take them out of the oven.

Choc Toblerone mousse

Yield: 4 serves

Ingredients:

2 cups milk

85g packet chocolate instant mousse

100g Toblerone chopped

Whipped cream to serve

Method:

1. Place milk into a medium bowl.
2. Sprinkle over mousse powder and prepare according to packet directions.
3. Fold 2/3 chopped Toblerone through.
4. Spoon mousse into 4 serving glasses.
5. Refrigerate for 15 mins to set.
6. Serve topped with dollop of whipped cream and remaining chopped Toblerone.

Baked custard

Yield: 4 serves
Ingredients:
1 cup milk
1 tbsp caster sugar
1 tsp vanilla essence
1 egg yolk beaten
2 cups water

Method:

1. Preheat oven to 180oC.
2. Mix milk, sugar and vanilla together.
3. Add beaten egg yolk and stir to combine.
4. Pour into 4 ramekin dishes.
5. Place ramekins in a pan filled with 2 cups of water.
6. Bake for 15-20 mins or until set.

Apple cinnamon muffins

Yield: 10 serves

Ingredients:

1 cup wholemeal self-raising flour

1 cup self-raising flour

½ cup brown sugar

½ cup apple sauce

2 egg whites

1 cup grated apple

¾ tsp bicarb soda

2 tsp cinnamon

Topping:

3 tsp sugar

1 tsp cinnamon

Method:

1. Preheat oven to 200oC.
2. Beat eggs and sugar for 1 min.
3. Stir bicarb and apple sauce together.
4. Add apple and gently fold in flour and cinnamon until combined.
5. Line a muffin tray with patty pans and pour mixture into each one.
6. Cook for 20 mins.
7. When cooked and hot brush a little water over the top and sprinkle with topping.

Tim tam truffles

Yield: 24 balls
Ingredients:
1 packet of tim tams
4 tbsp cream cheese
200g dark chocolate melts

Method:

1. Line a tray with baking paper.
2. Place tim tams into a blender or food processor and process until light crumbs and a few chunks.
3. Add the cream cheese and process until combined there should be no traces of white.
4. Using a teaspoon roll into 24 balls, place on tray and refrigerate.
5. In a bowl melt the chocolate melts stirring every few seconds until melted.
6. I melt mine in either the microwave or in my bluestone pan on low until melted.
7. Pour chocolate in a large bowl.
8. Using forks dip the tim tam balls into the melted chocolate and allow excess chocolate to drip away.
9. Place back onto tray when all coated and refrigerate to set.

Coconut rough slice

Yield: depends on how big you cut into squares

Ingredients:

1 tbsp cocoa powder

1 cup self-raising flour

1/3 cup caster sugar

1/3 cup desiccated coconut

125g melted butter

Topping:

2 tbsp cocoa powder

1 cup desiccated coconut

1 ½ cups icing sugar

½ cup sweetened condensed milk

1 tbsp butter softened

1 tbsp boiling water

Method:

1. Preheat oven to 170oC.
2. Grease and line a rectangular slice tin with baking paper and set aside.
3. Sift the cocoa and self-raising flour in a large bowl.
4. Add the caster sugar, desiccated coconut and melted butter and mix well together.
5. Press the mixture into the prepared baking tin and bake for 20 mins or until slightly firm on top.
6. Allow to cool.
7. Make the topping by placing the cocoa powder, desiccated coconut, icing sugar, sweetened condensed milk, softened butter and boiling water into a large bowl and mix well.
8. Use a hot knife (dipped in hot water then wiped off) to spread the topping over the cooled slice.
9. Place into the fridge to set before cutting into slices.

10. Store in an airtight container in the fridge for up to 1 week or freeze for 1 month.

Apple tea cake

Yield: 8-10 serves

Ingredients:

200g butter softened and chopped

¾ cup caster sugar plus 2 tsp extra

3 eggs

1 tsp vanilla extract

1 ¼ cups self-raising flour

½ cup plain flour

½ tsp cinnamon plus ½ tsp extra

¼ cup lemon juice

2 small apples cored and finely sliced

Custard or cream to serve

Method:

1. Preheat oven to 180oC.
2. Lightly grease and line a 20cm round springform cake pan with baking paper.
3. In a large bowl using an electric mixer beat butter and sugar together until pale and creamy.
4. Add eggs one at a time beating well after each addition.
5. Beat in vanilla.
6. Sift combined flours and cinnamon into a bowl and fold into creamed mixture with juice.
7. Spoon into pan smoothing the surface,
8. Arrange apple slices over top overlapping slightly.
9. Sprinkle with combined extra sugar and cinnamon.
10. Dot with extra butter.
11. Bake for 50-55 mins until cooked when tested.
12. Turn onto wire rack to cool completely.
13. Serve in slices with custard or cream.
14. Store in an airtight container.

Cranberry and orange icy poles

Yield: 8 serves

Ingredients:

100g frozen cranberries

1 cup caster sugar

2 cups cranberry juice

¾ cup orange juice

Method:

1. Place berries in a saucepan, use a potato masher to lightly crush.
2. Add sugar and juice and bring to a simmer.
3. Stir to dissolve sugar.
4. Cool.
5. Pour into icy pole moulds and freeze overnight.

Big freckles

Yield: make them as big as you like

Ingredients:

450g milk chocolate melted

1 cup 100's and 1000's sprinkles

Method:

1. Line a flat baking tray with baking paper and set aside.
2. Pour tablespoons of melted mixture or however big you want them onto the tray and cover with 100's and 1000's.
3. Place in the refrigerator or freezer to harden.
4. Peel off the baking paper and keep in a cool place.

Strawberry and cream bliss cake

Yield: 8 serves

Ingredients:

395g tin sweetened condensed milk

200ml thickened cream

200g strawberries hulled

Method:

1. Grease and line a 20cm round cake pan with baking paper.
2. Using an electric beater, whisk condensed milk and thickened cream until soft peaks form.
3. Pour into prepared pan.
4. Using a blender puree the strawberries and spoon over the top of the cream mixture.
5. Swirl into cream mixture using a fork and cover with cling wrap and freeze overnight.

Mum's chocolate slice

Yield: 24 serves

Ingredients:

185g butter melted

1 ½ cups brown sugar

1 egg

1 tsp vanilla

¾ cup plain flour

1/3 cup self raising flour

1/3 cup cocoa powder

¾ cup desiccated coconut

Icing:

1 cup icing sugar mixture

¼ cup cocoa powder

20g butter melted

Hot water

2 tbsp desiccated coconut for sprinkling over the top

Method:

1. Preheat oven to 180oC.
2. Beat together the butter, sugar, egg and vanilla then stir through the sifted flours and cocoa with the coconut until well combined.
3. Pour into a greased and lined slice pan.
4. Bake for 25-30 mins or until cooked through.
5. Sift the icing sugar mixture with cocoa powder into a bowl then stir in the butter and enough water to make a spreadable icing.
6. Spread over the slice and sprinkle with extra coconut.
7. Slice and serve once icing has set.

Subway cookies

Yield: 18 cookies

Ingredients:

2 cups self-raising flour

170g butter melted

1 cup brown sugar firmly packed

½ cup white sugar

1 tbsp vanilla essence

1 egg

1 egg yolk

2 cups dark chocolate chips

Method:

1. Preheat oven to 165oC.
2. Line 2 cookie trays with baking paper.
3. Sift the flour and set aside.
4. In a medium bowl, cream together the melted butter, brown sugar and white sugar until well blended.
5. Beat in the vanilla, egg, and egg yolk until light and creamy.
6. Mix in the sifted ingredients until just blended.
7. Stir in the chocolate chips by hand using a wooden spoon.
8. Drop big round tablespoons of the dough onto the prepared trays leaving plenty of room for spreading.
9. Bake for 15-17 mins in the preheated oven or until edges are lightly toasted.
10. Cool on baking tray for a few mins before transferring to wire racks to cool completely.

Double chocolate pancakes

Yield: 4 pancakes

Ingredients:

1 ¼ cups plain flour

¼ cup cocoa powder

3 tbsp white sugar

¼ tsp salt

2 eggs at room temperature

1 ¼ cups milk

½ tsp vanilla

40g butter melted

½ cup dark chocolate chips

Method:

1. Whisk flour, cocoa powder, sugar and salt together in a large bowl.
2. Beat eggs, milk, and vanilla in another bowl and mix in melted butter.
3. Pour the wet ingredients into the dry and mix just until combined.
4. Stir in chocolate chips.
5. Heat a lightly oiled frying pan over a medium-high heat.
6. For each pancake pour ¼ cup batter into the frying pan and cook until bubbles pop in the centre of the pancake about 2-3 mins.
7. Flip and cook an additional minute on the other side.

Quick Nutella mousse

Yield: 2-4 depending on size of serving glasses

Ingredients:

100g dark chocolate chopped

300ml thickened cream chilled

½ cup Nutella

Crumbled Cadbury flake to serve

Method:

1. Place dark chocolate in a heatproof bowl over a saucepan of simmering water.
2. Stir with a metal spoon for 3-4 mins or until chocolate just melts.
3. Set aside to cool slightly.
4. Use an electric mixer to beat the cream in a large bowl until soft peaks form.
5. Add the Nutella and whisk until the mixture is just combined.
6. Add the melted chocolate and use a large metal spoon to gently marble.
7. Spoon mousse evenly among serving glasses.
8. Sprinkle with flake and serve immediately.

Ultimate mars bar slice

Yield: cut into what size you like

Ingredients:

5 53g mars bars coarsely chopped

50g butter

¼ cup golden syrup

4 cups rice bubbles

200g milk chocolate melted

3 53g mars bars extra thinly sliced

Method:

1. Lightly grease and line the base and 2 sides of a 20 x 30 slice pan with baking paper allowing the sides to overhang.
2. Stir the 5 chopped mars bars, butter and golden syrup in a saucepan over low heat until the chocolate melts and the mixture is smooth.
3. Stir in the rice bubbles.
4. Spoon the mixture into the prepared tin and smooth the surface.
5. Spread the milk chocolate over the slice, smooth surface and top with sliced mars bars and place in fridge for 2 hours or until set and cut into pieces.

Lemon slice

Yield: cut into whatever size pieces you like

Ingredients:

½ cup sweetened condensed milk

100g butter

200g granita biscuits

1 cup desiccated coconut

2 tsp finely grated lemon zest

Lemon icing:

2 cups pure icing sugar

20g butter softened

2 ½ tbsp lemon juice

Method:

1. Grease a slice pan and line the base and sides with baking paper with paper over the sides of the pan.
2. Place condensed milk and butter in a small saucepan over medium heat.
3. Cook stirring for 5 mins or until smooth and combined.
4. Remove from heat.
5. Using a food processor, process biscuits until fine crumbs.
6. Transfer to a bowl and add coconut and lemon rind.
7. Stir to combine and add hot butter mixture and mix well to combine.
8. Press mixture over the base of prepared pan.
9. Cover and refrigerate for 1 ½ hours or until firm.
10. To make the lemon icing, sift icing sugar into a bowl.
11. Add butter and lemon juice.
12. Beat with a wooden spoon until smooth and combined.
13. Spread icing over slice.
14. Stand at room temperature for 30 mins or until icing has set and cut into pieces and serve.

Strawberry muffins

Yield: 6 muffins

Ingredients:

1 cup self-raising flour

1/3 cup caster sugar

½ vanilla extract

1 egg

1 tsp ground cinnamon

40g butter

¼ cup strawberries chopped

¼ cup milk

Method:

1. Preheat oven to 200oC.
2. Grease a 6-hole muffin tray or 12-hole mini muffin tray also you could put in patty pans.
3. Sift flour into a medium bowl, add sugar then combine vanilla, cinnamon, egg, butter and milk.
4. Add chopped strawberries and stir until just combined.
5. Divide mixture into muffin tray and bake for 10-12 mins or until skewer comes out clean.

Milo drop balls

Yield: depends on the size you roll them into

Ingredients:

250g arrowroot biscuits

4 tbsp milo

400g sweetened condensed milk

1 ½ tbsp butterscotch schnapps

1 ½ tbsp Bacchus cream liqueur (dan murphy's sell this)

Method:

1. Line a baking tray with baking paper.
2. Place coconut into a flat bowl.
3. Place biscuits and milo in a food processor and mix until crumbs are fine.
4. Add condensed milk, cream liqueur and schnapps and mix well.
5. Use wet hands and roll into small balls.
6. Coat with coconut and refrigerate until firm.

Peppermint bubble slice

Yield: 24 pieces

Ingredients:

200g block peppermint chocolate chopped

180g dark chocolate chopped

50g copha

5 cups rice bubbles

3 35g peppermint crisp chocolate bars roughly chopped

Method:

1. Grease a slice pan and line the base and sides with baking paper.
2. Place peppermint chocolate, dark chocolate and copha in a saucepan over medium heat.
3. Cook stirring for 3-4 mins or until melted and smooth.
4. Place rice bubbles and peppermint crisp in a large heatproof bowl.
5. Add chocolate mixture and stir to combine.
6. Spoon mixture into the prepared pan, pressing down with the back of a spoon to level.
7. Cover and refrigerate for 2 hours or until set.
8. Cut into squares and serve.

Banana chocolate cake

Yield: 6-8 serves

Ingredients:

1 ½ cups wholemeal self-raising flour

¾ cup self-raising flour

2/3 cup cocoa powder

½ tsp bicarb soda

1 cup caster sugar

2 eggs lightly beaten

2 large bananas over ripe and mashed

¾ cup buttermilk

½ cup vegetable oil

Method:

1. Preheat oven to 180oC.
2. Lightly grease an 8-cup capacity, 24cm fluted ring tin.
3. Sift flours, cocoa and bicarb into a bowl.
4. Add husks from the sieve and add sugar and stir to combine.
5. Make a well in the centre.
6. Combine eggs, banana, buttermilk and oil in a jug and stir to combine.
7. Spoon cake mixture into tin and bake for 40-45 mins or until skewer comes out clean.
8. Stand cake for 5 mins to cool.

Berry sundaes with white chocolate sauce

Yield: 6 serves

Ingredients:

2 tbsp caster sugar

2 250g punnets strawberries hulled and sliced

200g fresh or frozen raspberries

2 litres vanilla ice cream

300ml pouring cream (can get at Woolworths)

250g white chocolate finely chopped

1 tbsp cognac or brandy optional

Method:

1. For white chocolate sauce, place cream in a saucepan and bring to an almost boil over a medium heat.
2. Remove from heat and add chocolate and stir until smooth and melted.
3. For an adult twist stir in the alcohol.
4. Transfer to a jug then refrigerate until sauce is chilled.
5. Process sugar, and ½ the strawberries in a food processor until smooth.
6. To serve place a few raspberries and a few remaining sliced strawberries in the base of your serving glass, top with scoops of ice cream and a few more berries.
7. Drizzle with a little strawberry sauce and white chocolate sauce.
8. Repeat with remaining berries, ice cream and sauces in the other 5 glasses and serve immediately.

Banana and buttermilk cake

Yield: 6-8 serves

Ingredients:

200g softened butter

1 cup caster sugar

3 large eggs

1 cup mashed banana

2 tsp vanilla extract

1 cup buttermilk

1 ¾ cup self-raising flour

1 tsp bicarb soda

Pinch of salt

Method:

1. Preheat oven to 180oC.
2. Lightly grease a 23cm springform cake tin and line the base with baking paper.
3. Cream the butter and sugar until light and fluffy.
4. Add eggs, mashed banana, vanilla and buttermilk.
5. Sif the flour, bicarb and salt into another bowl and stir to combine.
6. Mix the flour mixture into the batter and mix until smooth.
7. Pour into the prepared tin and bake for 45 mins or until a skewer comes out clean.
8. Cool in the tin for 10 mins and then turn out onto a wire rack and cool for 10 mins more.
9. Serve warm with cream.

Double chocolate muffins

Yield: 6-12 serves

Ingredients:

¼ cup cocoa powder

¼ cup boiling water

3 cups self-raising flour

¾ cup caster sugar

1 cup chocolate chips

1 egg beaten

1 ½ cups evaporated milk

125g butter melted and slightly cooled

Icing sugar for dusting

Method:

1. Preheat oven to 190oC.
2. Grease muffin tins or place patty pans into muffin tins.
3. Mix sifted cocoa and boiling water together to make a smooth paste and allow to cool.
4. Sift flour and sugar into a large bowl and add chocolate chips.
5. In a separate bowl mix together the cocoa mixture, egg, evaporated milk and butter.
6. Make a well in the centre of the dry ingredients and add milk mixture.
7. Stir until just combined.
8. Spoon batter into prepared tins and bake for 20 mins.
9. Serve dusted with icing sugar.

Triple choc muffins

Yield: 6-12 serves

Ingredients:

50g milk chocolate chips

50g butter

2 eggs

1/3 cup caster sugar

1/3 cup self-raising flour

1 ¼ tsp cocoa powder

25g white chocolate chips

Method:

1. Preheat oven to 180oC.
2. Melt milk chocolate chips with the butter in a small pan over a low heat.
3. Beat eggs, sugar, flour and cocoa powder in a large bowl.
4. With a metal spatula fold in the melted chocolate mixture and white chocolate chips.
5. Spoon the mixture into a muffin tray lined with patty pans and bake for 12 mins or until risen and firm to the touch.
6. Transfer to a wire rack to cool slightly before eating.

Strawberry tarts

Yield: 4 serves

Ingredients:

250g punnet strawberries hulled and sliced

¼ cup icing sugar

1 tsp orange zest

½ tsp ground cinnamon

1 sheet puff pastry thawed

1 egg white lightly beaten

Sugar to sprinkle

Icing sugar, cream or ice cream to serve

Method:

1. Preheat oven to 200oC.
2. Line an oven tray with baking paper.
3. Place berries in a bowl.
4. Sprinkle with icing sugar, zest and cinnamon and mix well.
5. Cut pastry into 4 rounds using a cutter.
6. Pile berry mixture into centre.
7. Pleat pastry around the edges and brush with egg white and sprinkle with sugar.
8. Bake 12-15 mins until puffed and golden.
9. Dust with icing sugar and serve with cream or ice cream.

OTHER RECIPES

Easy sausage rolls

Yield: 20 pieces

Ingredients:

1 packet puff pastry

1 packet sausage mince

2 carrots peeled and grated

1 onion diced

Plain flour

Method:

1. Preheat oven to 180oC and line a baking tray with baking paper.
2. Thaw out pastry on the bench while you make your filling.
3. On a cutting board add some plain flour to the board so the mixture won't stick.
4. Open the sausage mince and put on top of the flour.
5. Add carrots and onion to the sausage mine and use your hands to mix together.
6. Once all combined cut your pastry in half and spoon some of the mixture in the middle of the pastry.
7. Fold over pastry on one side and the same on the other.
8. Cut into 4 pieces and put on baking tray.
9. Once all the sausage rolls have been made and on the baking tray cook for about 30 mins or until golden.
10. I do turn them over halfway through.

Lemon butter

Yield: 1 jar

Ingredients:

115g butter

½ cup sugar

3 eggs well beaten

Juice of 3 lemons

Method:

1. In a small saucepan melt the butter.
2. Add sugar, eggs and lemon juice.
3. Cook over a gentle heat until thick.
4. Pour into a jar and store in fridge.

Zucchini slice

Yield: 6-8 serves

Ingredients:

2 zucchinis grated

250g diced bacon

1 red capsicum diced

1 green capsicum diced

1 brown onion diced

6 eggs

1 cup shredded cheese possibly more sometimes I add up to 1 ½ cups

1 cup self-raising flour

Method:

1. Preheat oven to 180oC.
2. Grease and line a baking tray.
3. In a big bowl mix all ingredients together except for the flour.
4. Slowly pour in some of the flour and mix that through then continue adding flour until all combined.
5. Pour mixture into the prepared pan and bake for 35-40 mins or until golden on top.

Shakshuka

Yield: 4 serves

Ingredients:

1 brown onion thickly sliced

500g packet tri colour capsicum, thinly sliced

2 400g cans diced tomatoes

4 eggs

½ cup parsley leaves

Method:

1. Heat a large non-stick frying pan over a medium-high heat.
2. Add the onion and capsicum and cook, stirring occasionally for 5-10 mins or until onion softens.
3. Add the tomato and cook stirring for 5 mins or until mixture boils and thickens slightly.
4. Use the back of a spoon to make 4 large indents in the tomato mixture.
5. Carefully crack an egg into each indent.
6. Reduce heat to low.
7. Partially cover the pan and cook for 10 mins for soft yolks or until eggs are cooked to your liking.
8. Sprinkle with parsley leaves to serve.

Spinach, feta and ricotta pie

Yield: 4-6 serves

Ingredients:

½ cup plain flour

1 cup ricotta cheese

½ cup feta cheese crumbled

2 cups milk

4 eggs lightly beaten

2 cups baby spinach blanched

¼ cup parmesan cheese grated

Method:

1. Preheat oven to 180oC.
2. Lightly grease a pie dish.
3. Sift flour into a mixing bowl.
4. Stir in ricotta and feta.
5. In a jug blend together milk and eggs.
6. Whisk flour mixture with spinach.
7. Pour mixture into pie dish.
8. Sprinkle evenly with parmesan.
9. Bake for 45-50 mins or until lightly golden and set.
10. Serve warm or cold with a salad.

Croque monsieur

Yield: 2 serves

Ingredients:

30g butter

1 tbsp plain flour

½ cup milk

125g gruyere cheese grated

4 slices woodfired bread

1 tsp Dijon mustard

100g sliced ham

Method:

1. Melt the butter in a saucepan over low heat.
2. Add flour and cook for 1-2 mins without letting the mixture brown.
3. Add milk and continue to cook over low heat for 4-5 mins or until thick.
4. Add half the grated cheese stirring to combine.
5. Set aside to cool.
6. Spread 2 slices of the bread with Dijon mustard, place ham and remaining cheese on top and cover with another piece of bread.
7. Place on a baking tray and grill the sandwiches under a hot grill on one side.
8. Remove sandwiches from the grill turn over and spread with ungrilled side with cheese sauce return to the grill and cook until golden brown and bubbling.

Easy cheesy muffins

Yield: 12 serves

Ingredients:

2 cups self-raising flour

2 cups shredded cheese

2 cups milk

Butter for greasing

Method:

1. Preheat oven to 180oC and great a 12-cup muffin tray.
2. Place all ingredients in a large bowl and mix well.
3. Spoon evenly into prepared tray and bake for 30 mins or until skewer comes out clean.
4. You can also add diced ham, chicken, tomato, capsicum, mushrooms, pineapple, grated carrots, spring onions or even a packet of french onion soup mix if you are looking for different flavours.

Pizza toast

Yield: 1 serve
Ingredients:
1 slice of bread
Pizza sauce
2 slices of ham
Handful of cheese

Method:

1. Toast the bread.
2. Once toasted put on a plate and spread some pizza sauce on the toast.
3. Place ham and cheese on top and put in microwave for about 45-60 secs or until cheese melts.

Tuna melt

Yield: 1 serve
Ingredients:
1 slice of bread
1 can of sweet chilli tuna or whatever tuna you like
Handful of cheese

Method:

1. Toast the bread.
2. Once toasted put on a plate and spread some pizza sauce on the toast.
3. Place ham and cheese on top and put in microwave for about 45-60 secs or until cheese melts.

Chicken Noodle Frittata

Ingredients:

1 75g packet chicken noodles

1/3 cup frozen peas

1 tsp olive oil

3 eggs lightly whisked

Method:

1. Break the 2 min noodles into 3cm pieces.
2. Place in a heatproof bowl.
3. Add the flavour sachet from the packet of noodles and add frozen peas.
4. Cover with boiling water and set aside for 2 mins or until tender.
5. Drain and preheat the grill on medium.
6. Heat olive oil in a 20cm base frying pan over a medium heat.
7. Add the noodle mixture to the pan. Pour over eggs and cook for 3 mins or until set around the edge but still runny in the centre.
8. Place the pan under the grill and cook for 3 mins or until set.
9. Cut into quarters and serve.

Rice and capsicum

Yield: 4 serves

Ingredients:

Beef or chicken strips

1 red capsicum diced

1 green capsicum diced

1 large onion diced

2 large tomatoes diced

1 cup cooked rice

Some water or olive oil

½ tsp salt

Method:

1. In a frying pan brown, the chicken or beef strips first in a little water or oil.
2. Add capsicums, onion and tomatoes in the same frying pan and add salt and let simmer for 30 mins or until tender.
3. Combined cooked rice with the mixture and serve.

Mozzarella and prosciutto quesadillas

Yield: 2 serves

Ingredients:

4 flour tortillas

8 tbsp pizza sauce

100g grated mozzarella

4 slices of prosciutto diced

Method:

1. Preheat oven to 180oC.
2. Line a baking tray with baking paper.
3. Lay 2 tortillas side by side on the prepared baking tray.
4. Spread with 4 tbsp pizza sauce on each.
5. Sprinkle each with equal amounts of the grated mozzarella and diced prosciutto.
6. Lay the remaining two tortillas on top of the prepared tortillas.
7. Bake in the oven for 10 mins or until the cheese is melted and the tortillas golden brown.
8. Cut into quarters and serve.

Popcorn bags

Yield: 6 serves

Ingredients:

1 cup popcorn kernels

6 brown paper bags

Method:

1. Place 2 tbsp popcorn kernels into each bag and fold the top of the bag over 3 times then fold in the corners to secure.
2. Place 1 bag at a time in the microwave on high for 2 mins.
3. Use a tea towel to carefully take each bag from the microwave as they will be hot.
4. Allow to cool a little before you open them.

Tomato and zucchini sauce

Yield: 4 serves

Ingredients:

1 tin diced tomatoes blended

½ zucchini

1 large onion

½ tsp salt

Method:

1. Chop zucchini, and onion until diced.
2. Add tomatoes that have been blended and add salt.
3. Place in the microwave.
4. Serve with mashed potatoes and vegetables.

Garlic feta dip

Yield: 8 serves

Ingredients:

200g feta cheese

300g sour cream

80g low fat natural yoghurt

2 garlic cloves peeled

¼ tsp freshly ground black pepper

Method:

1. Combine the feta, sour cream, yoghurt and garlic in a food processor or blender.
2. Pulse briefly until garlic is minced.
3. Spoon into serving dish and season with salt and pepper.

Chocolate icing with evaporated milk

Yield: 12 serves

Ingredients:

2 ¾ cups icing sugar

6 tbsp cocoa powder

6 tbsp butter at room temperature

5 tbsp evaporated milk

1 tsp vanilla essence

Method:

1. In a medium bowl sift together the icing sugar and cocoa and set aside.
2. In a large bowl cream, the butter until smooth then gradually beat in sugar mixture alternatively with evaporated milk.
3. Blend in vanilla.
4. Beat until light and fluffy.
5. If necessary adjust consistence with more milk or sugar.

Zucchini pickles

Yield:

Ingredients:

1kg zucchini grated

½kg onion sliced

1 cup vinegar

2 tsp mustard

1 cup sugar

½ tsp turmeric

2 tsp curry

2 tsp salt

1 tbsp cornflour

Method:

1. Add zucchini, onion and vinegar in a pot and bring to the boil then reduce heat and simmer for 40-50 mins.
2. Add all remaining ingredients except cornflour and stir for 5 mins.
3. Thicken with cornflour and continue to stir.

Wholemeal pizza dough

Yield: 2 pizza bases

Ingredients:

7g sachet dry yeast

1 tsp caster sugar

1 cup wholemeal plain flour

1 ¼ cups plain flour

1 tsp sea salt

1 tbsp olive oil

Method:

1. Place yeast, sugar and1 cup warm water in a jug.
2. Whisk to dissolve yeast.
3. Stand in a warm place for 10 mins or until frothy.
4. Sift flours into a large bowl.
5. Add salt, yeast mixture and oil.
6. Mix to form a soft dough.
7. Turn out onto a lightly floured surface.
8. Knead for 5-7 mins or until smooth or elastic.
9. Place in a large, oiled bowl.
10. Cover and set aside in a warm place for 1 hour or until doubled in size.
11. Using your fist punch down centre of the dough.
12. Turn onto a lightly floured surface and knead for 20 to 30 secs or until smooth.
13. Divide dough in half and roll out each half into 25cm rounds.
14. Place rounds on 2 greased pizza trays with your choices of toppings.

Loaded cheesy bacon dip

Yield: 12 serves

Ingredients:

300g plain Greek yoghurt

1 cup shredded cheese

2 rashers cooked bacon

3 tbsp fresh chives

Salt and pepper to taste

Method:

1. Mix the yoghurt with the cheese, bacon, chives and salt and pepper to taste.
2. Mix well together.
3. Spoon into a serving bowl and serve with raw vegetables like carrot and celery or potato chips or crackers.

Baked eggs in ham cups

Yield: 4 serves

Ingredients:

12 slices of ham

12 eggs

Salt

Pepper

Paprika

Method:

1. Preheat oven to 180oC.
2. Line a muffin tray with slices of ham.
3. Crack an egg into each muffin spot and season with salt and pepper and paprika.
4. Bake for 20 mins.
5. Allow to cool for 3 mins remove slowly from the muffin tray and enjoy.

Healthy devilled eggs

Yield: 6 serves

Ingredients:

6 large, boiled eggs

3 tbsp fat free mayo

3 tbsp Dijon mustard

2 garlic cloves crushed

1 tsp salt

1 tsp pepper

1 tsp onion powder

Method:

1. Cut each egg in half, removing the yolks into a large bowl.
2. Using a fork, mash the yolks until they are small and granular.
3. Add remaining ingredients and stir to combine.
4. Scoop back into egg halves.

Jam pinwheels

Yield: 12 pieces
Ingredients:
2 sheets puff pastry defrosted
1 cup jam

Method:

1. Preheat oven to 180oC.
2. Line a baking tray with baking paper.
3. Lay out defrosted puff pastry sheets and cover each evenly with jam.
4. Roll up tightly into a sausage shape and using a pizza cutter slice each pastry sausage into 6 pieces.
5. Place each pinwheel onto the baking tray seam side down and bake for 20 mins or until golden and puffed.
6. Remove from oven and allow to cool.

Kid friendly turkey balls

Yield: 4 serves

Ingredients:

500g turkey mince

1 medium onion finely diced

1 zucchini grated

1 carrot grated

1 cup panko breadcrumbs

2 eggs beaten

½ cup mixed herbs

1 cup grated cheese

1 tbsp olive oil

Serve pasta

Sauce:

250ml tomato pasta sauce

420g can tomatoes

1 tbsp olive oil

4 garlic cloves minced

Method:

1. Mix onion, turkey, carrot, and zucchini together.
2. Combine egg, breadcrumbs, cheese and herbs into the same bowl as vegetable and turkey mixture.
3. Roll into small balls.
4. Add olive oil to frying pan over medium heat and cook for 5-7 mins or until cooked through.
5. Meanwhile simmer tomatoes, in a small amount of olive oil with garlic and pasta sauce.
6. Bring pan of water to the boil and cook pasta as per packet instructions.
7. Once all cooked serve pasta with turkey balls and cover with the sauce once reduced.

Ham and pineapple pinwheels

Yield: makes 24

Ingredients:

2 sheets puff pastry thawed

450g crushed canned pineapple

4 tbsp tomato paste

8 slices deli ham

100g mozzarella shredded

Cooking spray

Method:

1. Preheat oven to 220oC.
2. Spread tomato paste over the pastry sheets leaving approximately 1cm gap at the top end of the pastry.
3. Top with ham, then pineapple and cheese.
4. Gently but firmly roll up like a jam roll, rolling the pastry towards the end with the gap and place the join underneath.
5. Cut roll into approximately 1 ½ cm slices.
6. Place cut side down on an oven tray pre-sprayed with cooking oil, allowing a small amount of room for each one to spread.
7. Cook for approximately 15 mins or until golden.

Garlic potato

Yield: 4 serves

Ingredients:

4 large potatoes peeled and cut into 1cm slices

1 ½ cups mozzarella cheese

2 garlic cloves crushed

1 cup sour cream

Method:

1. Preheat oven to 180oC.
2. Lightly steam potatoes for 15 mins or until soft.
3. Combine 1 cup mozzarella, garlic and sour cream in a bowl.
4. Line a baking dish with ½ the steamed potato the top with ½ cream mixture and remainder of potato.
5. Alternate between layers with cheese and cream.
6. Top with remaining cheese and bake for 30 mins.

Zucchini fritters

Yield: 2 serves

Ingredients:

2 eggs

¼ red onion grated

½ zucchini grated

2 tbsp carrot grated

Method:

1. Beat eggs and add remaining ingredients and season with salt and pepper to taste.
2. Heat a small non-stick frying pan over a medium heat.
3. Spoon 2 x 2 tbsp mixture into the pan leaving room for spreading and cook for 2 mins each side.

Butterscotch sauce

Yield: 1 cup
Ingredients:
50g butter
Few drops of vanilla extract
100ml cream
¼ cup boiling water
¾ cup soft brown sugar
¾ cup caster sugar

Method:

1. Dissolve caster sugar in a saucepan over a gentle heat and bring to the boil.
2. Cook until syrup turns a golden brown.
3. Take pan off heat then pour in boiling water and stir.
4. Stir in the brown sugar and butter and return to the heat until mixture is smooth, and sugar is dissolved.
5. Stir in the vanilla and cream and cool until ready to serve.

GLUTEN FREE RECIPES

| 245 |

GLUTEN FREE RECIPES

Chocolate panna cotta

Yield: 4 serves

Ingredients:

300ml cream

200g good quality dark chocolate chopped

½ sachet gelatine

1 tsp vanilla essence

Method:

1. Grease 4 x ½ cup ramekins and place on baking tray.
2. Place cream in a small saucepan.
3. Stir over moderate heat 1-2 mins or until just boiling.
4. Remove from heat, stir in chocolate until nice and smooth.
5. Mix gelatine into 2 tbsp boiling water and stir until dissolved.
6. Cool slightly.
7. Stir gelatine and essence into cream mixture.
8. Pour into prepared moulds.
9. Cover with cling wrap and chill for at least 4 hours.

Sticky mango rice

Yield: 6 serves

Ingredients:

1 cup short grain rice

½ cup white sugar

1 ½ cups coconut cream

3 mangoes peeled and sliced

Method:

1. Place rice with 1 ¾ cups of water into a saucepan and bring to the boil.
2. Reduce heat, cover and cook for approximately 10 mins.
3. Add sugar and 1 cup of coconut cream stirring until combine and rice is nice and soft.
4. Dollop mixture into serving bowls and serve with mango drizzled with remaining coconut cream.

3 ingredient pumpkin soup

Yield: 4-6 serves

Ingredients:

750g pumpkin peeled and thinly sliced

1.25L gluten free chicken stock

1 large brown onion sliced

Method:

1. In a large saucepan, combine all ingredients.
2. Gently bring to the boil over a medium heat.
3. Reduce heat, cover and simmer until pumpkin is tender 20-25 mins.
4. Blend until smooth.

Alfredo

Yield: 4 serves

Ingredients:

¼ cup butter

1 cup heavy cream

1 cup freshly shaved parmesan cheese

200g fresh gluten free fettucine

Salt and pepper for seasoning

Method:

1. When boiling the pasta, melt butter in a large pan and add cream and bring it to the boil.
2. Simmer for 5 mins stirring constantly.
3. Add ¾ cup parmesan cheese and season well.
4. Reduce heat, add drained pasta do not rise and toss until thoroughly coated.
5. Serve with remaining parmesan.

Parsnip rice

Yield: 6 serves

Ingredients:

2 large parsnips peeled and grated

1 tbsp tahini

1 tbsp soy sauce

2 tbsp rice vinegar

Method:

1. In a bowl combine all the ingredients and mix well.
2. Cover and let stand for 15 mins then with clean hand massage together to create a rice like resemblance.
3. Serve over salad as a side dish to a salmon or tuna dish.

Country bbq pork ribs

Yield: 4 serves

Ingredients:

2kg pork ribs

2 large onions

1 garlic clove crushed

1 bottle of your favourite gluten free bbq sauce

Method:

1. Place ribs in the bottom of a slow cooker.
2. Add onions, garlic and gluten free bbq sauce.
3. Cover and cook on low for 7-8 hours.

Rich tomato pork

Yield: 4 serves

Ingredients:

4 pork chops

2 garlic cloves crushed

420g tin diced tomatoes with basil

½ cup cream

Method:

1. In a non-stick frying pan, fry the pork chops until golden on both sides.
2. Add garlic and tinned tomatoes.
3. Bring to the boil then let simmer for 2 ½ hours possibly more depending on the size of the chops.
4. Half an hour before serving, add cream and turn up the heat to thicken.
5. Serve with mashed potatoes.

Broccoli and lemon risotto

Yield: 2-4 serves

Ingredients:

1 bunch of broccoli

1 cup arborio rice

1 lemon

½ cup fresh grated parmesan

Method:

1. Steam the broccoli florets until barely tender.
2. Julienne the broccoli stems and sauté until tender.
3. Cook the rice in 1L of salty water stirring regularly until all the liquid is absorbed.
4. Grate the zest of the lemon onto the rice then add the juice of the lemon and ½ the parmesan.
5. Stir to mix, add broccoli and gently mix.
6. Season with salt and pepper.
7. Serve with remaining parmesan cheese.

Frittata

Yield: 4 serves

Ingredients:

6 eggs

3 cups freshly chopped spinach

1 ½ cup grated parmesan

½ cup gluten free breadcrumbs

Method:

1. Preheat oven to 150oC.
2. Beat the eggs with a whisk until light and fluffy.
3. Add spinach, cheese and gluten free breadcrumbs and season to taste.
4. Line a baking tray with baking paper.
5. Pour in mixture and cook for 20 mins.

Spinach pie

Yield: 2 serves

Ingredients:

2 cups shredded spinach

250g cottage cheese

1 garlic clove crushed

2 eggs whisked

Method:

1. Preheat oven to 180oC.
2. Boil spinach for 5 mins, drain and then in a small ovenproof dish layer spinach, cottage cheese and garlic.
3. After each layer spoon over a little egg.
4. Continue until all ingredients are used ensuring final layer is cottage cheese then season with cracked pepper.
5. Bake for 20 mins or until pie is slightly brown on top.

Mustard and thyme chicken breasts

Yield: 2 serves

Ingredients:

2 chicken breasts halved

¼ cup raw honey

¼ bunch fresh lemon thyme

2 tbsp gluten free wholegrain mustard

Method:

1. Preheat oven to 180oC and line a baking tray with baking paper.
2. Flatten the chicken breasts.
3. Spread with honey and mustard.
4. Place thyme sprigs in the middle of the breast allowing some of the leaves to hang over one end.
5. Roll up and secure with toothpicks.
6. Place on the baking tray, season with salt and pepper and bake for 20 mins basting halfway through.

Baked rice custard

Yield: 4 serves

Ingredients:

1/8 cup rice

¾ cup condensed milk

3 eggs lightly beaten

¼ cup sultanas

Method:

1. Preheat oven to 180oC.
2. Cook rice in a large pan of boiling water for 10 mins, drain.
3. Combine condensed milk, eggs, rice and sultanas with 1 ¾ cups water and mix thoroughly.
4. Pour into a shallow ovenproof dish.
5. Stand dish in a baking pan with enough hot water to come half-way up sides of dish.
6. Bake for 40 mins or until set.

Chocolate mousse

Yield: 2 serves

Ingredients:

2 avocados

1 banana

1 cup raw cacao powder

½ cup pure maple syrup

Method:

1. Scoop the pulp out of the avocado into a food processor, add banana, cacao and maple syrup and blend until smooth.
2. Spoon into glasses and enjoy.

DRINK RECIPES

Homemade lemonade

Yield: 4 serves

Ingredients:

1 cup lemon juice

2 cups water

¾ cup caster sugar

1 lemon thinly sliced

Method:

1. Combine lemon juice, water and sugar in a medium saucepan over a low heat.
2. Cook stirring for 5 mins or until sugar dissolves.
3. Remove from heat.
4. Transfer to a jug and add lemon.
5. Place in the fridge to chill.
6. Serve.

Frozen berry frappe

Yield: 8 serves

Ingredients:

2 500g frozen mixed berries

1L cranberry juice

2 tbsp honey

Method:

1. Place half the berries, cranberry juice and honey in a jug of a blender and blend until smooth.
2. Transfer to a large serving jug.
3. Repeat with remaining berries, cranberry juice and honey.
4. Serve immediately.

Berry punch

Yield: 4 Litres

Ingredients:

125g blueberries

125g raspberries

250g strawberries hulled and sliced

1.5L raspberry and cranberry juice chilled

1 cup vodka

1 lime

1.25L lemonade chilled

Ice cubes to serve

Method:

1. Place blueberries, raspberries and strawberries in a large bowl.
2. Add juice and vodka.
3. Cover and refrigerate for 1 hour to allow flavours to develop.
4. Thinly slice lime.
5. Cut slices into small wedges.
6. Stir through punch.
7. Add lemonade and ice.
8. Serve.

Cranberry and orange iced tea

Yield: 8 serves

Ingredients:

1 small orange

4 English breakfast tea bags

1L boiling water

1L cranberry juice

2 tbsp caster sugar

Method:

1. Use a vegetable peeler to peel the rind from the orange.
2. Use a small sharp knife to remove the white pith from the rind.
3. Place the rind and the tea bags in a large heatproof jug.
4. Pour over the water.
5. Set aside for 20 mins.
6. Remove the tea bags and rind and discard.
7. Add the cranberry juice and sugar to the jug and stir to combine.
8. Cut half the orange flesh into small pieces and divide among 2 ice cube trays.
9. Pour tea mixture among the trays.
10. Place in freezer overnight.
11. Cover the remaining tea mixture with plastic wrap and place in the fridge to chill.
12. Remove the ice cubes from the trays and place in serving jug and pour over the tea mixture and serve.

Pineapple and passionfruit soda

Yield: 8 serves

Ingredients:

1 ¼ cup unsweetened pineapple juice

¼ cup lemon juice

1 ¼ cups caster sugar

3 passionfruits halved

2L soda water chilled

Ice cubes to serve

Method:

1. Place pineapple juice, lemon juice and sugar in a saucepan over medium-low heat.
2. Cook stirring for 5 mins or until sugar dissolves.
3. Increase heat to high and bring to the boil.
4. Reduce heat to medium-low and simmer for 15-20 mins or until slightly thickened.
5. Remove from heat.
6. Stir in passionfruit pulp and cool.
7. Pour into a bottle or jug.
8. Refrigerate, covered for 30 mins or until chilled.
9. Add 2 tbsp fruit syrup to each glass and top with soda water and serve with ice.

Nightime dreamy relaxation drink

Yield: 1 serve
Ingredients:
1 cup milk
1 tsp honey
2 drops vanilla extract
1 pinch ground cinnamon or cinnamon sugar

Method:

1. Pour milk into s microwave safe mug and place into the microwave.
2. Cook on high until milk Is very hot and begins to foam, so about 3 mins.
3. Stir in honey, and vanilla then sprinkle with cinnamon before serving.

Banana smoothie

Yield: 4 serves

Ingredients:

2 large bananas coarsely chopped

2 cups milk

1 tbsp honey

2 scoops vanilla ice cream

Method:

1. Blend all ingredients together in a food processor or blender until smooth.

Grape berry bang

Yield: 2 serves
Ingredients:
2 cups red grapes
½ cup cherries pitted
½ cup strawberries
½ cup blackberries
Ice cubes optional

Method:

1. Place all ingredients in a blender.
2. Blend until combined.
3. For extra chill add a couple of ice cubes.
4. For a calcium boost add some low-fat natural yoghurt.

Butterscotch hot chocolate

Yield: 2 serves

Ingredients:

2 cups milk

100g good quality dark chocolate coarsely chopped

½ cup butterscotch schnapps

Marshmallows to serve

Method:

1. Place the milk in a small saucepan over medium heat for 5 mins or until almost boils.
2. Remove from heat and divide the chocolate among 2 heatproof glasses.
3. Pour over the hot milk and butterscotch schnapps.
4. Top with marshmallows to serve.

Classic cosmopolitan

Yield: 1 serve
Ingredients:
2 shots vodka
1 shot Cointreau
1 tsp lime juice
½ cup cranberry juice

Method:

1. Place ice in a martini glass.
2. Shake vodka, Cointreau, lime and cranberry juice in a cocktail shaker to combine and strain into the glass.

Pineapple daiquiri

Yield: 6 serves
Ingredients:
1 ½ cups pineapple juice
1 cup Bacardi rum
½ cup Cointreau
½ cup lime juice
Ice cubes

Method:

1. Place all ingredients into a blender and shake well until combined.
2. Strain and pour into glass to serve.

Lime and ginger breeze

Yield: 8 serves
Ingredients:
Crushed ice to serve
4 large limes juiced
2 litres ginger beer chilled

Method:

1. Chill 8 glasses in freezer.
2. Before serving spoon ice into each glass.
3. Combine lime juice and ginger beer in a large jug.
4. Stir to combine and pour into glasses and serve.

Jungle juice

Yield: 2L

Ingredients:

½ medium pineapple peeled and cut into 2cm cubes

750ml bottle soda water chilled

2 cups orange juice chilled

¼ cup lime flavoured cordial

Method:

1. Place pineapple in a large serving jug.
2. Add soda water, orange juice and cordial.
3. Stir to combine.
4. Serve.

Choc mint hot chocolate

Yield: 8 serves

Ingredients:

½ cup cocoa powder sifted

1/3 cup caster sugar

8 cups milk

½ tsp peppermint essence

Marshmallows or mini marshmallows to serve

Method:

1. Combine cocoa and sugar in a jug.
2. Whisk in milk and peppermint.
3. Transfer mixture to a saucepan over medium heat.
4. Cook stirring for 6-7 mins or until almost boiling.
5. Pour into mugs and top with marshmallows and serve.

Berry and banana milkshake

Yield: 1 serve

Ingredients:

2 cups milk

2 large scoops vanilla ice cream

1 medium banana peeled and chopped

1 cup frozen mixed berries

1 tsp vanilla extract

Method:

1. Blend milk, ice cream, banana, berries and vanilla together until smooth.
2. Pour into chilled glasses and serve.

Breakfast slushies

Yield: 10 serves

Ingredients:

2 pineapple peeled and chopped

2 250g punnets strawberries hulled and chopped

6 passionfruits pulp removed

4 limes juiced

2 425 cans apricot nectar chilled

3 cups crushed ice

Method:

1. Blend pineapple and strawberries in batches until smooth.
2. Pour into a large jug.
3. Stir in passionfruit pulp, lime juice and apricot nectar and mix well.
4. Fill each of the glasses with 1/3 serving glass of ice.
5. Pour over fruit mixture and serve.

Banana blast

Yield: 4 serves

Ingredients:

2 bananas

1 cup milk

3 tbsp water

1-2 tbsp brown sugar

8 ice cubes

Method:

1. In a blender combine bananas and milk.
2. Pulse until bananas are chopped.
3. Pour in water and brown sugar.
4. Blend until smooth.
5. Toss in ice cubes and blend until smooth and pour into 4 glasses and serve immediately.

Apple citrus crush

Yield: 1-2 serves
Ingredients:
2 oranges zested
2 cups apple juice
2 cups fresh orange juice
Ice cubes

Method:

1. Zest skin of 2 oranges and put aside.
2. Combine all other ingredients in a jug and then add zest and stir to combine.
3. Serve.

CHRISTMAS RECIPES

Chilled passionfruit cheesecake

Yield: 12 serves

Ingredients:

1 250g packet Arnott's buttersnap cookies

100g butter melted

2 tbsp hot water

1 tbsp gelatine powder

9 passionfruits halved

2 250g packets cream cheese at room temp

1 cup thickened cream

¾ cup caster sugar

Method:

1. Line a 16 x 26cm slab pan with non-stick baking paper.
2. Place the biscuits in a food processor and process until finely crushed.
3. Add the butter and process until well combined.
4. Use a large spoon to spread and press the biscuit mixture into the base of the pan.
5. Cover with clingwrap and place in fridge for 30 mins to cool.
6. Meanwhile place the water in a heatproof bowl and sprinkle with the gelatine.
7. Place the bowl in a saucepan and add enough boiling water to the pan to come halfway up the side of the bowl.
8. Stir until the gelatine dissolves and set aside to cool slightly.
9. Place the passionfruit pulp in a fine sieve over a bowl and use the back of a spoon to press the juice from the pulp into the bowl (you will need 1/3 cup passionfruit juice).
10. Reserve the pulp and seeds.
11. Use an electric beater to beat the cream cheese, cream and sugar in a bowl until smooth.
12. Beat in the passionfruit juice.

13. Beat in the gelatine mixture.

14. Pour into the prepared tin.

15. Spoon the reserved pulp over the cheesecake mixture.

16. Use a flat bladed knife to swirl the pulp through the mixture and tap the pan on the bench a few times to settle the mixture and place in fridge overnight to set.

Chocolate and raspberry trifle

Yield: 8 serves

Ingredients:

1 320g packet assorted biscuits omitting the melting moments crushed

2 300g packets frozen raspberries thawed

½ cup marsala

500g mascarpone at room temp

½ cup caster sugar

3 eggs separated

2 45g flake chocolate bars roughly broken to serve

Method:

1. Place biscuit in a glass bowl.
2. Reserve ¼ cup of the raspberries.
3. Sprinkle the raspberries over the biscuit and drizzle with 100ml of marsala.
4. Use an electric beater to beat the remaining marsala, mascarpone, sugar and egg yolks in a bowl until combined.
5. Use a clean electric beater to whisk the egg whites in a clean, dry bowl until soft peaks form.
6. Use a metal spoon to fold egg whites in the mascarpone mixture until just combined.
7. Pour over the raspberries and smooth surface with the back of the spoon.
8. Cover with cling wrap and place in fridge for 8 hours to set.
9. Sprinkle trifle with chocolate and reserved raspberries to serve.

Decadent chocolate custards

Yield: 4 serves

Ingredients:

Basic custard:

300ml pure cream

300ml milk

6 egg yolks

2 tbsp cornflour

1 tsp vanilla bean paste

1/3 cup caster sugar

Chocolate top:

50g 70% dark chocolate chopped

1 tbsp brandy

Chocolate curls to garnish

Method:

1. For the basic custard combine cream and milk in a medium saucepan over a medium heat and bring to a simmer.
2. Meanwhile whisk the egg yolks, cornflour, vanilla and sugar together in a large heatproof bowl.
3. Gradually whisk in the hot cream mixture until smooth.
4. Return mixture to cleaned saucepan and place over low heat.
5. Cook stirring constantly until custard thickens and thickly coats the back of a spoon and set aside to cool slightly.
6. For the chocolate top divide the custard evenly between 2 heatproof bowls.
7. Add chopped chocolate into one bowl and stir until well combined and smooth.
8. Add brandy to second bowl and stir until well combined.
9. Cover surface of both bowls with cling wrap to prevent a skin from forming.
10. Set aside to cool then refrigerate until chilled.

11. Divide chocolate custard evenly between 4 serving glasses then top with the layer of brandy custard.
12. Garnish with chocolate curls to serve.

Christmas trifle

Yield: 6 serves

Ingredients:

4 aeroplane jelly strawberry jelly crystals

2 ½ cups boiling water

½ 800g light fruit cake cut into 3cm cubes

2 tbsp brandy

2 cups Pauls double thick french vanilla custard

1 cup fresh raspberries or frozen raspberries

125g fresh strawberries hulled and sliced

300ml thickened cream

1 tsp icing sugar mixture sifted

50g white chocolate grated to decorate

Fresh raspberries to decorate

Hulled quartered strawberries to decorate

Method:

1. Place jelly crystals in a heatproof bowl and add boiling water and stir to dissolve crystals.
2. Stir in 400ml cold water and refrigerate for 1 hour or until just starting to set.
3. Arrange cake in a 13-cup capacity serving bowl.
4. Drizzle with brandy and spoon half the jelly over the top.
5. Top with custard.
6. Sprinkle with raspberries and strawberries and then spoon over remaining jelly over the top and refrigerate and cover overnight.
7. Using an electric mixer beat cream and sugar together in a bowl until soft peaks form.
8. Fold through chocolate and spoon over trifle.
9. Top with raspberries and strawberry quarters and serve.

Mixed berries in raspberry sauce

Yield: 4 serves

Ingredients:

2 punnets raspberries

¼ cup orange juice

½ cup caster sugar

1 tbsp orange liqueur

2 punnets strawberries

1 punnet blueberries

Method:

1. Put 1 punnet of raspberries into a saucepan with the orange juice.
2. Heat until juices begin to run.
3. Add sugar and stir over the heat until it dissolves.
4. Remove from heat and push mix through a sieve while hot.
5. Discard the pips and add liqueur to the liquid.
6. Leave to cool.
7. Hull the strawberries and place in a large bowl with the blueberries and remaining raspberries.
8. Add the raspberry sauce and mix gently.
9. Chill for at least an hour.

Candy cane and brownie ice cream

Yield: 2 litres

Ingredients:

2 litres vanilla ice cream

100g chocolate brownie (just get a store bought one) roughly chopped

8 candy canes coarsely crushed

Method:

1. Place a 2L metal container in the freezer until ready to use.
2. Scoop the ice-cream into the bowl of an electric mixer and beat on low speed for 1-2 mins or until softened.
3. Add the brownie and ¾ of the crushed candy canes and fold to combine.
4. Spoon into the chilled tin.
5. Sprinkle the ice cream with the remaining candy cane and freeze for 3-4 hours or until set.

Minted roast lamb and vegetables

Yield: 8 serves

Ingredients:

2.5kg leg of lamb

2 tbsp Dijon mustard

2 garlic cloves crushed

2 tsp sea salt flakes

2 cups water

800g baby carrots scrubbed

1 tbsp butter chopped

½ cup mint jelly

1 tbsp honey

Method:

1. Stand lamb at room temperature for 30 mins.
2. Preheat oven to 180oC.
3. Rub lamb all over with mustard, salt and garlic.
4. Season with freshly ground black pepper.
5. Place lamb on a wire rack in a medium baking dish.
6. Add the water to the dish.
7. Roast lamb for 1 ½ hours.
8. Meanwhile trim the carrots leaving the tops on.
9. Place the carrots on a large oven tray and spread butter on top.
10. Roast on a separate shelf with lamb for 30 mins or until tender.
11. Microwave half the jelly in a small microwave safe bowl for 20 seconds or until melted.
12. Brush lamb with the jelly.
13. Roast lamb for a further 1 hour for medium to well done or to your liking.
14. Brushing again halfway through with the jelly.
15. Cover lamb loosely with foil and stand for 15 mins.
16. Drizzle carrots with honey and toss to coat.

17. Slice lamb and serve with remaining mint jelly and carrots.

Pulled maple Christmas ham

Yield: 10 serves

Ingredients:

2kg leg ham on the bone scored

1 tbsp wholegrain mustard plus extra to serve

¼ cup lightly packed brown sugar

¼ cup maple syrup

2 tbsp dry sherry

Method:

1. Use a small sharp knife to cut around the shank of the ham about 10cm from end.
2. Carefully run the knife under the rind around the edge of the ham.
3. Carefully run your fingers between the rind and the fat to lift the rind in 1 piece.
4. Score the fat in a diamond pattern.
5. Spread ham with mustard and sprinkle with sugar.
6. Place in slow cooker.
7. Pour in the maple syrup and sherry.
8. Cook on high for 5 hours, turning once or twice during the cooking or until the ham is tender enough to be shredded.
9. Transfer ham to a platter and gently shred.
10. Transfer the cooking juices to a small saucepan and simmer over medium heat for 8 mins or until reduced and sticky.
11. Drizzle ham with the glaze and serve with extra mustard.

Choc-coconut Christmas balls

Yield: 50 balls roughly but depends on the size you make them

Ingredients:

250g packet plain sweet biscuits

180g dark chocolate chopped

395g can sweetened condensed milk

1 ½ cups desiccated coconut

100g packet red cherries chopped

Method:

1. Line a tray with baking paper.
2. Process biscuits until mixture resembles fine crumbs.
3. Transfer to a bowl.
4. Pour chocolate in a microwave safe bowl.
5. Microwave on for 1-2 mins stirring with a metal spoon every 20 seconds until smooth.
6. Add chocolate, condensed milk, ½ cup coconut and cherries to biscuit.
7. Mix to combine.
8. Place remaining coconut in a bowl.
9. Using damp hands roll 1 level tablespoon mixture into a ball.
10. Toss in coconut to coat.
11. Place on prepared tray.
12. Repeat with remaining mixture and coconut.
13. Refrigerate until set.

Christmas crackles

Yield: about 20 depending on size

Ingredients:

2 cups rice bubbles

50g butter

1 cup white marshmallows

30g white chocolate melts, melted

20 Jaffa's

Method:

1. Place rice bubbles in a large bowl.
2. Combine butter and marshmallows in a small saucepan and melt over low heat until smooth.
3. Pour onto rice bubbles and stir to combine.
4. Spoon mixture into mini patty pans and leave to set for 20 mins.
5. Spoon white chocolate over the crackle and place a Jaffa on top of each one.
6. Leave to set.

Gingerbread shapes

Yield: depends on the cookie cutter you use

Ingredients:

50g olive oil margarine

1 ¼ tbsp brown sugar

1 tbsp golden syrup heated

1 tsp ginger

100g self-raising flour

Icing to decorate

Method:

1. Preheat oven to 180oC.
2. Mix all ingredients until a dough forms.
3. Roll out on floured surface.
4. Using cookie cutters, cut out shapes in dough.
5. Bake for 12-15 mins or until golden.
6. Decorate with icing.